Saratoga Days

Saratoga Days

A LOOK INSIDE RACING'S GREATEST MEET

SEAN CLANCY

S_T

STEEPLECHASE TIMES PUBLISHING ❖ DELAWARE

Manufactured in the United States of America by Blaze I.P.I.
ISBN: 0-97025600-0
First Edition
1   3   5   7   9   10   8   6   4   2

Direct any inqueries to Steeplechase Times Publishing
P.O. Box 905, Newark, Delaware 19715-0905

For Michelle, the first to understand me.

$\mathcal{A}$cknowledgments

Saratoga Days was a dream of mine, one that flashed through my head as I walked out to the track atop Succeed on an early summer morning. Like always, my idea needed some wheels. From start to finish, the wheels kept turning. Thanks to all of you who believed. Dad for teaching me the difference between "good" and "well". Mom for teaching me when to use "good" and when to use "well". "Chainsaw" Joe for making this literate and me sane. Sheila for taking so many steps with me. Brian for taking so many steps with Sheila. Sam for the "are you really going to follow through with this?" talk. (Yes.) Ryan, Jack, and Keegan for the laughs. Annie for convincing me to do more than ride horses. *The Backstretch* magazine, Sam and Kevin in particular, for believing in my idea. The O'Briens for allowing me to fire myself halfway through the meet. Lizzie for letting me be late to the barn every morning. Chip for the confidence. Jack and Sheila for riding a writer. Barbara for the images. Kevin for the late-night scans. Blaze for mocking deadlines. Crambo for the goodness. Mig for telling me to give Ridley one in 1994. Buddy and Kate for keeping the light on. Keith for the company. Deirdre for wading into the darkroom. Jay for the example. Carolyn for telling me to write a book back in high school. Mike and Patrice for including the jumping set. Wass for the speed. Tugger for the comfort. Jen for the deciphering. Mark and the Wolfsons for going along with the jumping experiment. Pete for being a fan of horse racing and the book. Frank for the Genny Cream Ale. Tod for the editing. Pinkie Swear for trying. Cage, Red, and Student for the carpet rides. Succeed for showing me greatness. And most of all Saratoga for being Saratoga.

Saratoga Days

Hokan—on the perfect stride—flies the last jump in the 1998 New York Turf Writers Cup. *(Skip Dickstein)*

$\mathscr{P}$reface

I see it. Right there. A hundred yards away and I recognize it like my written name. The long stride.
Hokan makes the same discovery. We accelerate with
every move and nail it, soaring through the air together.

The perfect jump. The greatest feeling in the world.

There is a split second that decides that perfect jump in a steeplechase race. I rode Hokan around the turn at Saratoga as hard as I
could ride a horse.

Straightening for home, I pause to see when the last fence is coming. I don't stop riding, but freeze enough to see that perfect stride.
Or at least that's what I'm looking for; sometimes that perfect stride
never shows and no-stride-at-all is the only thing I see. The perfect
stride is when my horse reaches the fence without having to slow
down, and he can accelerate and launch off the ground in a long
powerful motion, making up time in the air. The perfect stride
means I win the race; the no-stride-at-all means falling on my head.

The one moment of hesitation comes when I'm trying to see what
stride my horse is going to be on when we reach the fence. Sometimes I see it a long way out. This was one of those times. I saw it, the
most amazing sight. I wouldn't trade the sight of the long stride at
the last fence at Saratoga for the view from the top of the world.

Man, what a view.

I saw it on Hokan in the biggest race of my life.

Somehow I knew it was coming.

This race was in slow motion. Horses running 30 mph and jumping 12 fences for 2⅜ miles don't go in slow motion. Riding steeple-

chase races is bump and run, clip and shake, pinball in the dark.

Maybe the moon was full and the planets were lined up and my guardian angel was on duty, but something was different this time.

I woke up at Saratoga that morning like every other morning, hungry, tired, grouchy, but otherwise it was Sean Clancy at Saratoga. Then I rode the race, and everything slowed to a crawl. This was like looking down First Avenue in Manhattan and having all the cabs pull over and wave you on. All the lights are bright green. Pedestrians just stand on the corners and watch you drive down the street. Potholes are paved, the sun's at your back, the world is yours.

It's never happened before or since. I never could say I was ever in the zone. Maybe August 27, 1998—the $108,500 New York Turf Writers Cup—was my zone.

Hokan planted himself on the inside of a seven-horse field. Just in touch, not too far out of it but not too close either. This race fit like a tailored shirt.

I was just watching and laughing.

Sundin's doing too much in front. Bisbalense just isn't that good. Prime Legacy doesn't matter. Chip is cruising on Romantic, I can tell by the way his ass sits way above the saddle. I'm going better than Clearance Code and the old champ Lonesome Glory is behind me; that's a good sign.

Don't ask why this is and don't change anything. This is holding sunshine in your hand. I have lightning, thunder, rain and wind in MY bottle.

I have a light hold of the reins, the stirrups fit like another layer of skin, and Hokan underneath me feels like the King of the World. Ron Turcotte never felt this on Secretariat.

Hokan was in the zone and I was with him. This was Michael Jordan in the fourth quarter of Game 7.

We were running too. As fast as two horses can run to the last fence (yes, I had company)—Hokan on the outside, Romantic on the inside—for the money and most important the vindication. I got the jump on Romantic and my friend Chip Miller going into the turn; I needed to, because they were going up the inner. I knew that yesterday.

I need the long jump, the if-you-give-me-this-one-I'll-never-ask-again jump. And there it is.

Hell, Hokan owed me.

I knew Hokan from a prior life. We met two years before this jump. He was a new member of trainer Leo O'Brien's stable. He was a 3-year-old man eater. He came with a reputation longer than his stride. Wouldn't train. Wouldn't eat. Wouldn't run. Certainly wouldn't win.

So my job was to ride Hokan, a son of French champion Trempolino. And fix him while I was at it.

I'd wake up in the morning and think about Hokan. I felt like a schoolteacher who has to face Johnny Troublemaker every day. He made my life miserable. Every single morning for six weeks.

We spent long days together. Some days it was Frazier and Ali. Occasionally, Romeo and Juliet.

He'd buck. Spin. Wheel. Bite. Kick. And I'd hang on and try to change his attitude. He got me once, bucked me off at the top of the backstretch baseball field, sent me flying on my head, and then in typical Hokan fashion, wheeled around and kicked me in the arm as I lay on the ground. That was Hokan.

My back still hurts from that day.

I jumped Hokan over his first fence. It was nothing like the last jump in the Turf Writers. I had to beg and cheat to ride the horse in the race. Steeplechase trainer Janet Elliot purchased the horse from O'Brien sometime between when he bucked me off and this race.

Elliot likes it when she has something other people want. This time it was Hokan. I was about the only jockey who wanted it, but I wanted it badly. For a jockey, watching the Turf Writers is an insult. It's the best steeplechase race of the Saratoga season. And I've watched plenty of them. I implored her about riding the horse for 14 straight days (steeplechase jockeys act as their own agents). All I got was a smile.

Eventually I raked her dirt shedrow with a giant metal rake to convince her how much I wanted the mount—a longshot in the season's most important race. She finally gave in and called me three days before the race. I'll never forget what she said: "You can ride the horse if you promise to be polite when you're wearing his silks."

I wanted to tell her to take Hokan and all her etiquette requests and . . . nobody tells Sean Clancy how to act. But I knew in my gut that she had a point.

I live in this frustrated why-can't-you-see-the-obvious-like-me? state. I would go off on Jesus Christ if he didn't see it my way. And I know that. Elliot was simply bringing up my reputation.

I said, "OK, Janet, I'll be good." Like swallowing a boot.

And I was. Whew, was I good. Finally.

Riding steeplechase races at Saratoga was simply losing steeplechase races at Saratoga for me. Three wins in 11 years will leave you disgruntled to say the least. This is all I ever wanted to be, a jockey at Saratoga. Growing up in the Clancy household meant you lived horses; being a jockey was like being president of the United States.

I love Saratoga but with that love comes a self-induced pressure to succeed, to give reason for my being there. And I always lose there.

I needed Hokan to change that.

I rode Hokan simply to have a ride in the race. Just so I could say "yes" when my friends asked me if I was riding the big race.

But riding the big race came with a price. At least when you have my build. I'm too big for a jump jockey. Hokan was supposed to carry 140 in the race, that means my tack and I should amount to 140 pounds. Tack can be slimmed down to about four pounds. Me, 136 pounds? Get the saw.

When I told Janet that I could do a legitimate 142 on Hokan, well, I was stretching the truth a little. I had been eating and drinking at Saratoga for four weeks. I sneaked over and got on the scale at the track. 150.

Well, that's when jockeys start searching. I stood on the scale and beat myself up for every calorie consumed and every mile not run. Can I really do this? Can I really lose 12 pounds in three days? Like any jockey staring at what looks like a weight impossibility, I wanted to bag it. But it's Saratoga. And Saratoga doesn't take baggers.

That's why I couldn't see the light.

On Thursday, the day of the race, I was still six pounds away. I galloped a couple of horses, and went to the sauna. I stayed there from nine in the morning until one in the afternoon. Sitting in the sauna for four hours takes you to the depths, especially when you walk in there dehydrated and exhausted. Your resolve, with the 2⅜-mile race still eight hours away, is tested. Your mental and physical mettle is stretched to depths you were not certain existed.

I walked out of the jocks' room to go take a nap. I thought I would go home and sleep for an hour and come back to ride the Turf Writers, the ninth of 10 races on the card. I walked out to Nelson Avenue and Lincoln Street. And I couldn't see the light.

I just stood at the intersection trying to see if the light was red or green. The sun was shining like an iron hand over my skull. I looked to see if cars were coming, couldn't tell. I rested my hand on the street pole and tried to clear my careening head. Eventually a woman walked past me and started across the street, and I followed her. I know she had to think I was a crackhead.

I took my nap. In a word, fitful. I kept waking up thinking I missed the race, while my mouth was as parched as a camel's.

I was back in the jocks' room at 3 p.m., two hours before the race.

When it was time to weigh in, I timidly stepped to the scales, praying that the arrow would by the grace of God stop at 142. I couldn't look—all I heard was an "OK" from Sal, the clerk of scales. That battle was won. I did 142. Legitimate would be a reach, but so would winning the agonizing race.

So I walked out to the paddock, trying to remind myself to be polite and hoping Hokan could emulate the 1969 Jets and pull off a miracle.

But I had the gods on my side. I had told Mr. O'Brien that morning, "You know, if there is such a thing as divine intervention, or getting your due, then Hokan will win the Turf Writers for me today."

The ever-optimistic O'Brien smiled from his chair and nodded. "I think he just might."

That was good enough for me. A devout Catholic, O'Brien prays for his tea to taste just right when you bring it to him from the track kitchen.

Maybe it was the gods who placed Hokan's legs at that exact spot

We—winning trainer Janet Elliot and I—tipped the scales. *(Skip Dickstein)*

on the Saratoga turf course that sent him to the last fence on that perfect stride. It sure as hell wasn't me.

I just kept him together from there to the wire. Chip was making inches up on me and the finish line was coming in yards. Down the lane, I knew I was a winner. Some races are so close, so desperate, you can't feel them until they're over. Some are so hectic you can't taste them until you're back in the room. This one was all over me as I pumped and sticked to the wire. I crossed the line and my whole life was worth it. There would never be another day that I could say I wasted my first 28 years of my life. Not one day to ever say I never did it. I could feel all that as Chip hollered at me on the turn.

"You won the Turf Writers. Buddy you won the Turf Writers."

Chip is my best friend and he was in my ear with his hand out in congratulations. I was thinking, why isn't he pissed? I'd be pissed if he beat me by a neck in the biggest race at Saratoga. But Chip knows. He's watched me struggle.

Ever have a friend who's better at everything than you are? Riding horses, getting girls, living life. Chip is that friend. He had been champion jockey two years before, me with a concussion and him with a trophy. At this moment on the turn, Chip was saying, "I know it's been hard having me as a friend, I beat you in a lifetime of one-on-one, but this is your time. And I'll enjoy it with you." Hence the best friend tag.

We did enjoy it. I pulled up Hokan on the backside and took a deep breath. I was tired; the sauna and the ride had made my lungs ache. I took a deep breath, the first one of the day. Hokan and I just stood for a moment on the backside. Horses feel the magnitude of the occasion. He knew, I knew.

In four minutes (4:12 to be exact—a track record) he made up for all the losing. You know when you finally accomplish something, you're glad for the struggle that preceded it all. The days of doubt and years of turmoil now make the success that much better.

We turned to go home, got a yell from Jonathan Kiser, who finished third on Sundin, and a couple of grumbled congrats from jockeys who knew they could have ridden Hokan. A couple of looks that said "How the hell did you pull that one out of your - - - ?" Hokan and I just smiled. We galloped back together, trying to savor one moment in time.

It was the longest, slowest gallop back to the winner's circle in my life. Just like the race, seconds were minutes, minutes hours. The Saratoga crowd started clapping for us. The same as they did for Holy Bull after he desperately staved off Concern in the 1994 Travers. The same tribute Fourstardave got for eight straight years. Quieter maybe, but not when you're under the helmet on the hallowed ground where Man o' War, Ridan and Jaipur, Go For Wand, your heroes and legends once bled their hearts. It's loud from there. So loud and so soothing. So amplified and so enveloping.

Hokan and I slowed to a jog, then a walk. As I've seen Richard Migliore do with Fourstardave and Angel Cordero Jr. do with Chief's Crown, I stood Hokan in toward the center of the universe. This is the time to hold it. The time to shut your eyes and take it in. The last time you're alone on this incredible horse in this incredible moment. Hokan just stood and stared out at the lake, the old wooden

Hokan heads to the winner's circle. *(Barbara D. Livingston)*

jockey board, the trees and the gazebo.

I gave him a pat and turned back to the crowd, back to the winner's circle, to the waiting hands of groom Leo Ayala, who had fed and rubbed and soothed the 5-year-old gelding every day for the past year of his life. Janet was there, her once spotless white pumps in the dirt of the track, smiling and wondering how it all happened. The warning about being polite was a distant memory. Owner Nancy Gerry, the lady who pays Janet $50 a day to make decisions like these, was still cheering on the edge of the track. She had the same smile and the same curiosity about our success. She looked at us first like, "How did this happen?" and then like "Who cares." Leo led us into the winner's circle where I hadn't been since 1994. It was just a chalk circle then, the greatest chalk circle ever drawn. Now it's a winner's circle with brick and trellis.

My older brother, the pillar of my being, is jumping and pumping his fist like he won the race, and in a way he did. A high-five from Joe on the way into the winner's circle at Saratoga.

Photos from Barbara Livingston, Skip Dickstein, Ellen Humes. I think Ansel Adams and Alfred Eisenstadt might have been in there, too. I put my hand on Hokan's neck like I've done a hundred times before on different horses for different photos, but never like this time. I smile and try to put my foot perfect for the camera.

As I jump off, I think of one more hurdle that needs to be jumped. I slide my one-pound, kangaroo skin saddle (from my dad's racing days) across my forearm, flip the two elastic girths over the top of the number cloth and wrap the half-pound elastic breastplate around the whole pile of tack. Then I sprint to the scales. When I told Janet "legitimate," it was a way of saying no cheating. In every racetrack in the country, jockeys "cheat" a little to do the weight. A weight assignment is a little like a speed limit: you can always hedge a hair or two above the number.

I sprinted and Janet's radar locked on to my bumper. I jumped on the scale, Sal said "OK" and I handed my tack to my valet, Snook, as I jumped off. Janet missed the scale number by a step. She's the only trainer in the world who would always remind you that you came back two pounds over and never remind you that you won the Turf Writers on a 15-1 shot. I grabbed her by the arms and smiled. She knew and I knew.

Somewhere amid all the festivities, I asked Janet, "Was that polite enough?" I just had to—you don't get many opportunities like that.

We stood for another photograph, this time with the silver trophy from the New York Racing Association.

I waited on the edge of the track to do an interview. A television audience had to wonder "What in the world is up with those jump jockeys—that boy didn't make a word of sense." It made sense to me.

I walked back to the jocks' room, still feeling polite in the blue-and-white silks of my now lifelong friend Hokan. I'll never forget the room. These people had been watching my tirades and sulks for all these years. They knew the climb and the pain I had put myself through for the last 11 years and they told me how psyched they were that I won the Big One. It felt so good.

It took me 20 minutes to get to my corner, another 20 to take off the polite silks, and my black plastic boots with the red tops took another 10 minutes as I talked and reveled in the experience.

This is why it's better to achieve after a struggle. There was a time when I wouldn't have noticed all this, wouldn't have felt it, wouldn't have bathed in it. Wouldn't have been able to write about it with such flurry.

I missed the traditional champagne toast in the Trustees' Room. I didn't care.

Finally a long shower, as the room was pretty much deserted. Home to my one-bedroom apartment to call Dad. The other pillar in my life. My greatest friend and supporter, the man who felt every bump in the road with me.

He was over-the-top in such a Dad way. Just quiet and so content. He had left me a message on my mobile phone: "Way to go Bud." We talked about me riding the race of my life and him watching it on the simulcast at Delaware Park. Of course, he had the $100 exacta, me over Chip, that was easy. I knew my 63-year-old father would sleep like a baby that night.

Chip, Keith O'Brien and I had reservations at the Lodge with Keith's family. We walked into the restaurant on the edge of the harness track like kings. Leo looked at me and said, "How about that, we knew it all along, didn't we?" in a mischievous, albeit sincere, Irish brogue.

I sat down in the first seat on the right of a long rectangular table. I looked at Leona Velazquez, whom I dated a little bit at Saratoga in 1989. She married John Velazquez, one of the top flat jockeys riding at Saratoga, several years later. It was the first time in my life I felt like career-wise I could sit at the same table as John Velazquez. For that one day, I was the big jock at Saratoga. I was the only jockey to win a stakes at Saratoga on Thursday, August 27, 1998.

Eating after dieting for a race is one of the greatest things you can ever do. Eating after winning the New York Turf Writers Cup that you dieted for, is heaven on earth. I had the fish special, grouper, I think. Drank a victory Sam Adams. We talked about Hokan off and on through dinner, I thought about Hokan on and on through dinner.

Walking out of the Lodge, they wouldn't even let me pay; I felt as light as air. An amazing feeling with a belly like a bed.

We went home to drop off the car before the night out. One

thing we've learned in our life at Saratoga—always walk.

So Joe, Chip, and I headed off to downtown Saratoga. Joe had been home writing a story about the race, still being big brother. We know all the shortcuts in Saratoga, over White Street, across Union, through Congress Park, past Ben and Jerry's to the Parting Glass, where the world awaits.

There were more fireworks in Saratoga. The town was having a fireworks display that would make our shortcut a longcut. We stepped over the menacing orange plastic fence, ducked under the yellow caution tape and were halfway through the park when Saratoga security stopped us. What? We won the Turf Writers, there are no barricades that apply to us. "Back up son, I never heard of the Turf Writers, never heard of Hokan and I've certainly never heard of you. Nor do I want to." Another lesson we've learned at Saratoga: stealing the Travers Canoe from the lake is one thing, but when a man has a badge on his chest and a gun on his hip, be polite and walk around the park. "Thanks for keeping us safe, Mr. Officer."

We made it to the Glass in two shifts. Somehow we got separated after I had to find the ATM machine (it was going to be a long and expensive night). I walked into the Glass. Norm never got a reception in Cheers like this.

I swung the door open and announced, "Let the games begin."

And they did.

Having a reason to party at Saratoga is like having your birthday fall on New Year's Eve on the night you get married on the last day of the war.

I walked to the bar and Frank, the bartender, congratulated me before I even said, "It's on me tonight."

Maybe it was just the inner confidence I felt from riding Hokan, but I simply enjoyed the world's company. People just seemed more entertaining, more inspiring than ever before. If somehow I could corral the self-worth I felt that night, the world would be in my palm.

I set up camp in the middle of the long bar in the front room of the Glass.

Sonny Via, who came to town to find out what I meant when I wrote "If you're in the game and you don't come to Saratoga, why are you in the game?" walked up with an empty glass and said "Now I know why I'm in the game." I thought, "You do and you don't." I asked what he was drinking. He said, in a word, "Beer." What kind, I asked. "Dark," in another word. It was that simple.

We raised the roof when the race replays came on the big-screen television in the corner of the bar. With each race, the crescendo was rousing. As the Turf Writers came on the screen, we went wild. The entire bar watched each jump, each furlong, like it was live in front of our eyes. This is the thing about Saratoga—it's like a giant private club. The whole town, in August, is horse racing. Everybody, and I mean everybody, is a fan for six weeks. The bartender congratulates you before you even tell him what you did today.

Saratoga is like March Madness. When secretaries who don't know a three-pointer from a three-way call toss 10 bucks in for the office pool. This is horse racing's March Madness, when all attention funnels into one pool.

I stood stunned, watching myself—this was the first time I had seen it—as the rest of the place slapped me around. I watched and thought, for the first time in my life as a jockey, I could really ride.

Hokan hit the wire a neck ahead of Romantic again. We high-fived again, clanked our glasses again, pumped our fists again.

Then jockey Phil Teator stood up and cut the celebration in half. "Wait, there's still one more race." And the place erupted, again. This is Saratoga—we knew what he meant—and we focused on the television again. Teator won the last race of the day on a huge long-shot named Quiet Caller. The place was in a frenzy when he hit the wire to complete the late double with me.

Teator and I were soul mates for a night. He was struggling at the meet, too. A young man trying to compete with the best in the business at the place that he dreamed about as a child.

We shared our wins with every person in the Glass—that's Saratoga. The one place where winning a race matters. People know when you win one at the Spa.

We closed the Glass, which is an achievement in itself. Off to Aiko's where we danced to a band playing everything from the Grateful Dead to Pearl Jam.

I'll never forget dancing in the dark, basement bar. How can winning one horse race make you feel like you can really dance? Amazing game, astonishing life.

I remember being told, "Sean, every time you dance with a girl, she ends up covered in your sweat. It looks like she took a shower." I answered, "And?"

Eventually we all made it home. In the excitement, my garage apartment had turned into Motel Six.

I climbed into bed and announced this revelation—"It's 4:48 and my alarm's set for 5:15. My man, Hokan."

So I got up 27 minutes later and passed Chip, me on my way to the track and Chip on the way to my bed.

I stepped over a floor of bodies and went to work.

It was play that day. I felt like a flower child. The world was beautiful—people and horses at peace and play. I said good morning to all of Saratoga that day.

Winning the New York Turf Writers Cup on Hokan was my best day of Saratoga. Life actually. Now hang on for more. These are the days of Saratoga.

Introduction

"All writers think they have a book in them. And that's where it should stay."

I read that somewhere before I started this book. You be the judge. This is not an attempt at literary genius, this is a book of passion. The passion for Saratoga and all the life that goes with it. I think you'll see what I mean.

Now that you just jumped the last fence of the 1998 Turf Writers Cup with me, we shall jump our way through Saratoga 1999.

The idea for a book about Saratoga Springs, New York, finally came into the active side of my brain around June 1999. I started coming to this incredible horse racing town in upstate New York in 1970, the year I was born, and haven't missed a summer yet. I think I've been writing a book from that first day, always looking, trying to preserve my take on what was happening around me. Like all writers, I believe if it's not written down it really didn't happen.

I saw Secretariat lose the Whitney in 1973 (the picture of the Clancy family—me in my seersucker sunsuit—standing railside with the Triple Crown winner cantering to the start lives indelibly in my memory), and I was in the grandstand for the Coronado's Quest–Victory Gallop–Raffie's Majesty Travers of 1998. Saratoga is the wildest, most unpredictable constant in my life. Come along for the ride. Sometimes I'll be driving, other times just another passenger trying to see out both windows. Saratoga can be I-95 or a winding footpath in the country.

I want this book to be the one essential read for everybody on their way to Saratoga. I want travel agents to read it and send customers to the "August place to be." I didn't originate the phrase but it sums up the place in one quick quote. Au-gust.

The adjective "august" means "inspiring awe; imposing" and "marked by majestic dignity or grandeur." Webster's doesn't use many photos, but Union Avenue in Saratoga Springs would work perfectly on page 64 of my dictionary.

Saratoga was the site of one of the most important battles in the Revolutionary War, when the British surrendered to the American troops. It was an implausible and critical victory for the battered and nearly beaten Colonials. Saratoga was where Man o' War lost his only race—to a horse called Upset. The place where the natural springs shoot up from the ground like magic. The place where tuxedos are worn like jeans. A place where, "I was at Saratoga," can serve as a valid excuse for trouble you found there. Wives, husbands, parents, bosses, judges have all heard that line of reasoning from a perfectly honest, albeit in trouble, Saratoga tourist.

Saratoga is the convergence of horses and people for six weeks during the middle of summer when anything goes. It's the best racing in the world. I'll argue Saratoga over Del Mar, Ascot, Chantilly, anywhere on the globe. The air just breathes in better at Saratoga. And the sun comes up brighter. The rain falls harder. The horses run faster. The *Daily Racing Form*, the horseplayer's bible, is sold on every corner. The people come alive at Saratoga. If you don't like it here, you won't like it anywhere.

I know Saratoga like a lover who will never sleep. The month of August at Saratoga is my time. She tempts me, caresses me, teases me; Saratoga is my challenge. I can't shake her, and I don't care to. She's that good.

She's the one in the elegant dress that glides across a room, beautiful and graceful, daring you to look at her and tempting you. She will dance with you, but only if you're bold enough to ask. And you might stagger off the dance floor, never the same. The spell will be cast.

Every year since 1988, I have spent the whole summer at Saratoga.

Mostly as a struggling steeplechase jockey. In 1999, I went as a struggling steeplechase jockey—and something different. "There's the guy who's writing that book," I hoped to hear.

The Internet was the appetizer. I wrote a journal entry every day from July 23 to September 7 on the *The Backstretch* magazine's Internet site (www.thebackstretch.com). You might have read some of what follows on the Net. It's better now. Slowed down. Organized.

This project started simply as an idea. It had no marketing survey, no business plan, no budget, no funding committee, no agenda, no rules. It was me, my laptop and Saratoga. I let the town, the days, decide what happened. The challenge was to see if informal rivers of Saratoga observations could hold a book together. But I live for such challenges. Correct spelling slows me down. Grammar, punctuation, paragraphs—ugh. I once typed "relostate" in a column and referred to the six-furlong "shoot" in another. Typed out "wha-la" once, too.

Long story short, there were no publishers' bids to sort through. This book lives because of the place, and the way people feel about it. This was simply an idea.

So find a tree to stretch out under or lie across your bed and drift away with Saratoga and me.

I grew up with horses. All I ever wanted to be was a jump jockey, even back when I was too scared to ride the pony and certain that I would be a steeplechase jockey when I grew up. Summer vacation for me was to come to Saratoga in the back of the horse van. Odd Man, Salvo, Hawaiki, Town And Country were my traveling companions.

My father, an old-time horse trainer, says he gets along better with horses than people. Me? Depends on the horse.

I've led horses to the paddock at Saratoga. I've bet horses at Saratoga. I've ridden winners at Saratoga. Fallen off at Saratoga. Worked for Hall of Fame trainers at Saratoga. Been fired by Hall of Fame trainers at Saratoga. Sat in the back of a police car at Saratoga. I've slept in mansions and in my Chevy Cavalier at Saratoga. I've been drunk, tired and alone at Saratoga. I've been alive, wild and in stellar company at Saratoga. I fell in love for the first time in Saratoga. I've listened to Rod Stewart, Jimmy Buffett, Joan Rivers,

Joe Hirsch, Marshall Cassidy, Jack Whitaker and Tom Durkin at Saratoga. And I'm not alone, Saratoga is Utopia for any person lucky enough to get there. Grooms making minimum wage and living in 10-by-12 rooms flock to Saratoga. Millionaires and billionaires come running when it's Saratoga time.

Like all those people, I've lived Saratoga. So many years later, the town still gets me. I wasn't born there nor have I ever lived more than six weeks at a time there. I still feel like a visitor, a guest of a miraculous town. I don't even know the zip code. But Saratoga is part of me.

I think about momentous occasions in my life, times of great joy and immense pain, and I think about Saratoga. I am tested at Saratoga. The six weeks (it used to be four) represent a condensed passing of time—like four years of college squashed into a semester.

The full-speed-ahead schedule takes you from a hot cup of tea as the sun comes up over the backstretch to sitting on a downtown curb eating pizza at three in the morning. All in one day for 42 consecutive days.

You can be on a horse's back at five in the morning. Maybe it's a future Saratoga legend like Fourstardave, maybe it's just another four-legged creature that fills out the last race of the afternoon.

The backstretch at Saratoga is as good as all those photos you see. Sun shining through the mist, horses rattling feed tubs, steam rising off a river of coffee. Mornings at Saratoga are like no other mornings in the universe. The nights aren't bad either.

Saratoga is the main character but also the setting or the scene. The stage if you will. The horses are the protagonists. The people are here because of the horses. They are also characters in the story, but they all have supporting roles.

No matter whom you meet at Saratoga, the horses top the list. They are the reason for it all. An innocent star who can't read the papers to know what he actually provides, the horse is king at Saratoga. From Amarettitorun to Zee Buck, the Saratoga horse will inspire, amaze, sadden and heighten you. The racehorse is the greatest star that has never been quoted in the history of the world. Right up there with the tree and the sun. The horse is a rare crea-

Good morning Saratoga days. *(Barbara D. Livingston)*

ture, one that can't hurt its reputation by saying something stupid.

Horses and horsemen. That's who we'll be and who we'll meet. Don't worry if the only horse you know is Mr. Ed and the horseman you are most familiar with is Roy Rogers; Saratoga is for everyone. My friend Chip Miller grew up on a horse, he loves Saratoga. My friend Paul Wasserman couldn't ride a carousel pony, he loves Saratoga.

As for me, I usually follow the same program—just take off and go during the last week of July. Pack up the car—it's been a '95 Honda Civic for the last four trips—and escape.

I gallop horses in the morning, ride steeplechase races two days a week, go to the races every day, go out at night, do anything that comes my way. Anybody going to Saratoga starts counting the days in May. Every time I think about retiring from being a jump jockey I think about Saratoga.

Rent a house. Apartment. Dive. I haven't rented the same place twice in 12 years. We won't go into why. Let's just call it plenty of lost security deposits. Lived with three girls in '89, seven guys in '90, upstairs from Penny Chenery in '94. I'll never forget the words of our landlord: "The boys were delightful but the hours they kept, and the noise they made . . ." I actually became quite good friends with Secretariat's mom.

In 1999, I staked claim to a house on Nelson Avenue with Keith O'Brien. Sure would be fun to do this for the next 50 years.

I wish I was doing this when I came to Saratoga in 1988, my first full season there. I slept on the floor. No air-conditioning. No bed. No money. I slept with an ice tray on my chest one night and in a full bathtub another. No joke. And, no, I was never cool.

Bureau Chief provided my first ride at the Spa. Most kids dream about Yankee Stadium or Boston Garden. I longed to be in uniform at Saratoga.

Imagine yourself standing at the plate with, say, Sandy Koufax on the mound. That's what it felt like to ride at Saratoga. Getting dressed a couple of feet from Angel Cordero. I was in awe, the horse was in awe and we were both overmatched. In one blink it was over. Finished third at 30-1. How I'll never know.

And you know, the "in-awe" feeling has never dissipated. Angel is no longer in the jocks' room, his ear-splitting Spanish music nothing but a memory, but the place is still the place. It's just different when you walk out of the jocks' room at Saratoga. Down the long alley from the room to the crowd. Pop your whip off the metal pipe that runs overhead, for that ping sound that means you are on your way out to ride at the greatest track in the world. Sign a couple of autographs, nod at the same Pinkertons guarding the walkway year after year. Amble into the tree-filled paddock where the greats have stood before you. Ooooh, it's Saratoga.

After my first stint, when I slept in the tub and rode three races, I knew I'd never leave. The next year, I actually found a job and air-conditioning.

Not that I really needed it. The air is crisp at Saratoga. You start feeling it as you drive up I-87. The town is less than six hours from my home but it's also another world. Saratoga is my vacation. My escape.

It can be yours, too.

Something's Missing

Saratoga 1999 took a shot in the knees early this year. For the last three years I have spent the best part of my mornings with a friend. He's my buddy. We laugh at the world together. His name is Amarettitorun. Read it again, out loud, syllable by syllable, Am-A-Retti-To-Run. Great name.

He's a tough little banger whom Leo O'Brien trained and I rode every morning. Leo ran him at Belmont Park early in the summer for $50,000 and trainer Gary Gullo claimed him. Saratoga without Amaretti will be like Disney World without Mickey.

I had thought of this book a day or two before he was to run. "Hey it will be cool to talk about my daily rides on Amaretti for the book," I told myself. He's everything a racehorse should be, except sound, fast and overly talented. What's he got? What we all need. Tenacity. He's overcome it all. I can't believe I won't hear my friend Keith, Leo's son and assistant trainer, tell me every morning, "Sean, Amaretti, do your thing." Our thing was our thing. It was better than a morning stretch, better than the sunrise, better than the morning paper.

We jogged two to three miles every day. I knew his every move and he knew mine. It was like getting up every day and having breakfast with an old friend. You know the way he takes his eggs, you know what you'll talk about. You know his opinions before he even says them. But it's still an irreplaceable part of your life.

Amarettitorun is a character, and that's what makes the racetrack so enthralling and so addicting. This horse is more entertaining than most people I know. Certainly has more resolve, more fight than the rest of the world.

Of course, he's a front-runner who runs every step like it's his last. You should see him run, knowing what you know. Last year he chased blue-blooded stakes horses Tale Of The Cat and Garbu. No matter who he faces, he tries to outrun them, and when they finally out-talent him, he'll look at you and say, "I tried and I know, I know damn well, they had a break, they took a shortcut, I know they can't beat me on the square."

Let yourself go, and trust me on that one.

He's got this great indentation on his face, right under his eye, where his skull formed around his leg when he was in the womb. It's a perfect imperfection that gives his face a distinct look. I'll miss that face.

My Saratoga friend Amarettitorun even took me to Hong Kong.

Yeah, I'm nuts over some horses. Amaretti is one. I don't know Gary Gullo, but I do have it in my mind to see if he'll want a freelance exercise rider for his new horse.

The tough part is I don't want to see anybody improve on Leo; he's my friend and a great boss, but it will kill me to see my other old friend get beat up. I'm not sure what I'll do when Amaretti hits the head of the stretch at Saratoga this year. Do I root for him? Part of me, I'm certain, will be with his every step.

I always have this vision. Maybe it's heaven, maybe it's after I sell a million copies of this book. It's my driveway. Tree-lined, miles and miles long. On both sides, all the horses who touched my life live in the greatest, shade-filled, stream-fed pond paddock. As I drive in and out, all my old friends hang their heads over the boards and give me a wave. Red Raven, Riverdee, Student Dancer, Woody Boy Would, Doubledarn, To Ridley, Bewray, Bee's Prospector, Contract Court greet me day and night. Yes, horses wave. Amaretti, I hope you have that great indented head looking at me one day.

NERVES

Saturday, July 24

Saratoga hasn't changed and maybe that's one of the reasons we like it so much; it never changes. It's like a childhood friend you see once a year: she looks the same, sounds the same, and you pick up right where you left off.

The town stands solitary and strong while we arrive year after year ready to feel its aura.

I left Pennsylvania at three in the morning, slept-drove all the way through New Jersey and arrived here around 8:30 so I could get on Succeed.

Guess you don't know about Succeed. Well, he is the greatest horse in the world—but only he and I know it. Right now. That's why I'm writing now, the night before his steeplechase debut. It all could be different around two tomorrow.

I have been training Succeed for nine months. His full sister is

Succeed was always
ready for Saratoga.
(Elizabeth Hendriks)

Flawlessly, the two-time Eclipse Award winner. Mark Hennig trained
him on the flat. I call Succeed my last project. At least, horse project.
He is my entire stable—I don't train horses for a living and never
want to, but sometimes one comes along to alter that desire. One
that puts a spell on me.

I started a book about Succeed but never kept it going. Like most
of my life, it's about half done.

Succeed is what I envision a spouse should be. For whatever reason, you think your spouse—your companion—is the greatest living
creature. Others think she is fine, but you think she walks on water.

That's how it is with Succeed and me. I can't speak for him—he
probably thinks I should sink to the bottom of the Atlantic—but I
know if I asked, he'd start gliding above the waves like the savior
himself. I swear we see everything the same way.

I'm nervous about tomorrow. Training horses well will break the
strongest man. Anybody can hang a shingle and call himself a
trainer, but to do it well, that is a challenge. There is always something more or different you could have done. I worry if he's
schooled enough, if I've made the right decisions. Basically, by tomorrow we will know if this is a good story or bad story. I'm a little
scared tonight.

I always get slightly nervous before I ride. More like on-edge. Over the last 12 years, riding races has become easier, but still the slight tenseness arrives on the night before a race. Tonight I'm nervous. And beyond on-edge. I've been over the edge since last Tuesday when I entered Succeed. I'm flat-stinking nervous about Succeed. I just had dinner at Bruno's, home of wood-oven pizza (I ate a salad) with Dad, Ricky and Lizzie Hendriks and Fenneka Worley. They are my pit crew with Succeed. They deserve the Nobel Prize for Patience after dealing with Succeed and me for the last year. But they aren't where I am tonight. I walked out of Bruno's and could see the outline of the grandstand. Tomorrow I'll be on the other side aboard Succeed awaiting the conclusion to a good story/bad story.

Have you ever sat at a dinner table and not heard the conversation, not even tasted the food? My head is in the sixth stall down in the first barn of the Oklahoma Annex way at the end of Fifth Avenue. Succeed seems so far away tonight.

I hope he handles everything. I hope the rest of the world sees what I see.

TESTS

Sunday, July 25

The Succeed story is a good one, not a perfect one, but good nonetheless. Like I said in my introduction, Saratoga tests me. I got tested today at the Saratoga Open House.

I have spent virtually every day for the last three months with Succeed. I woke up on Sunday morning and decided to make like a jockey and remove myself. I slept in. Never even went by the barn, just decided it was time to be a jockey and not a brother, father, friend. Riding a horse that I'm so attached to was the hardest thing I've ever done in my career. I have galloped, schooled, breezed Succeed to get here. I have scrubbed, massaged, iced Succeed to get here. I have cajoled, tutored, tempered Succeed to get here. It was finally showtime.

I had three rides at the Saratoga Open House, which serves as a preview a few days before the meet actually begins. Cinch, Mr. Chiclet and Succeed, in that order. That gave me all day to think about my man. I would have preferred to get it over with and ride him first.

Cinch started the day with a little of everything. He nearly won. He nearly fell. He nearly exhausted me. He nearly killed me.

Cinch is another old-timer with more heart than wheels. One of those horses who throws the switch on race day and gives you everything. You can feel him turn his body into grin-and-bear-it mode. Like a piston in an engine, except with feelings.

We got in front leaving the backside, slipped through the inside and opened up a big lead around the turn. I could feel him wavering a little as we rounded the turn. One more fence to go, I tried to steady him and meet the fence in stride; nothing happened. He just dragged himself through the top two feet of the hurdle. He landed back legs first, trying to keep the pressure off his front, and lost all his momentum and the lead to Cavasham and Dipiperon. I could feel his will shut down the pain and make his legs dig in. Gaining ground again, we passed Dipiperon and finished second through pure determination.

Cinch just emptied out when I stood up in my stirrups after the finish line. He started favoring one side and I tried to pull him up as soon as I could. It's like the weight of the world. We managed to stop without going over and I jumped off to ease his pain. This was Chris Antley and Charismatic, but without the national audience exposure.

Cinch wouldn't put his right front leg on the ground. Imagine being a 1,200-pound animal running 30 mph, fighting off the world and then stop. One leg no longer works like it used to. From breath-busting competition to solitary confinement in one instant. And without being able to verbally communicate and make logic of the stress.

It's brutal to put your mount on a horse ambulance and walk home alone. It's the toughest part about being a jockey—there is no lonelier place in the world—and I'm the lucky one. I think Cinch will be OK: he's in his stall now with a big bandage and a brace. They took X-rays and hopefully he can return to soundness one day. He will never race again, but he will make some pet.

The good part is he's still alive. He's in pain now, and the pain will go away. Unfortunately, he doesn't know that.

The day gets worse. My second ride was a horse named Mr. Chiclet. A gray 4-year-old who seemed perfectly nice. We were in front heading into the first turn when a horse behind us clipped the back of Mr. Chiclet's legs. The horse's metal shoe severed Mr. Chiclet's tendon. I knew something was wrong, he wasn't moving right, but it was hard to tell. I kept thinking he would get it together again, but after three more fences I knew he was in trouble. I was hoping he had grabbed his own shoe and it had changed his stride.

I kept going, like a fool, ignoring my gut, hoping for a miracle. Every time you ignore your instinct, you make a mistake. I put the horse through more pain because I couldn't trust my instinct that something was radically wrong. In my head I was hearing the rap I get sometimes for pulling horses up too soon. Just more proof that your gut knows.

Finally, I pulled him up and jumped off. His hind leg was a mess. No blood, just a slice across his tendon. He couldn't put any weight on it; the leg was useless. It was bending in a spot that was supposed to be straight.

He kept looking at me—for an answer I guess. Like he knew something was wrong and I was the only one he could find and he kept waiting for me to fix it. I couldn't do anything, just held on to the reins and tried to console him. All I could do was pet his neck and try to keep him still. Sometimes you hear that horses don't have feelings; that's BS. I swear he was looking at me like a son would look at his dad. Mary Laura Griggs-White, his trainer, ran up to me and I had to tell her. I wish it was just me pulling up a horse too soon. Not this time. She burst into tears and ran to her fallen project. Mr. Chiclet was her Succeed.

They put him on the horse ambulance and I went back to ride Succeed. Mr. Chiclet was dead in about, well I don't even know how long, but they put him down. I knew when I handed over the reins that it would be the last time I ever saw the horse. They gave him a fatal injection. I didn't know him very well; I had ridden him three times. It is easier when you aren't attached, but it's still the worst thing in the sport. I know it's a horse and it's part of the sport, but it was me down there who made the decisions that caused a life to end.

I had visions of this journal as the glorious time at Saratoga, the magic, the mystique, the festivities. Now here I am talking about my first two rides at Saratoga and the first two horses I said good-bye to.

None of you knew Mr. Chiclet or Cinch. Most of you never would have known it happened. I don't know if I should have written about them, and I also know stories like that don't put Thoroughbred racing in a positive light. But I'm writing a journal, not a brochure.

Now I am compelled to write about Succeed. Seems like it took a long time to get to him.

It's a major undertaking for a horse to run first time over jumps. He has never run this far in his life, 2⅟₁₆ miles, or jumped this many consecutive fences, 11.

Succeed hadn't raced in 14 months, so he had to overcome that obstacle as well. Anyway, he was second. He ranged up head and head to the last and jumped it OK. Just landed a little slow and lost his momentum. The more experienced Vinco just jumped more fluidly than he did. Succeed picked himself up and was still closing at the end.

It was cool. I felt like a father, teacher, coach and friend all at the same time. Yeah, jockey, too. I wish he could have won, but it was an amazing experience. Talk about tired. I had him as fit as I think I could have, but he was knackered by the end.

I still think he's the greatest horse in the world. Today made it all worth it. I can't help but think about how ecstatically I would be writing to you if he had won. Wow, do I wish he won.

You should have felt him hammering toward the first fence. We were all running to the hurdle and I'm not sure he was really expecting the jump to be there. He rose when he arrived at it but it was still a surprise rise.

He was a long way from the fence and I couldn't see the stride (as a jockey you are supposed to see or feel when the horse is going to leave the ground). Well Succeed just galloped to the first fence and soared over it. He left the ground earlier than I wanted and leapt at

Succeed launches over the first fence in his steeplechase debut.
(*Elizabeth Hendriks*)

it a little flat and boldly but we made it just the same. I kind of knew after he made it that everything would be fine.

He jumped the second fence more conservatively and then went exactly like I thought he would. Now I feel like a fool for doubting he would run like this.

The downer of it all is that I thought he was going to win and that I had a slight rider excuse. I wish I had waited a little as we turned for home. And if I had just let him reach the last on his own terms rather than looking for that Hokan-esque jump.

Ah well, hindsight will make you crazy. I just didn't want a jockey excuse.

The best moment of the day, mostly because I've learned to notice, was when I walked into the paddock to ride him. I put my first two horses on the ambulance and then came out to ride my project, my buddy. I walked out to the paddock, at Saratoga, and just stopped. Succeed was walking around the paddock, under the number one and two trees. I just stopped and took it all in.

He was walking, his coat was shining and he was totally calm, like he knew where he was, like he knew he belonged. Horses are so amazing when they show you how much class they have. How smart they are. This horse looked incredible. I'll never forget seeing Succeed walk around the paddock, just stopping to capture that moment. Harbor View Farm's flamingo, black and white silks that Affirmed wore in his Triple Crown were on my back. Kodak never had a moment like this one.

I know he only finished second in a maiden steeplechase, but that instant was worth everything.

WARMING UP

Monday, July 26

The place is grumbling. You can feel it. You should see the horse vans pulling in. The commercial fleets—Sallee, Ralph Smith, others you've never seen before. The vans barge through every stop sign of the town, every stable gate of the racetrack. It's like the players arriving off the plane for the big game. It's wild with horses—they climb off the van and you have no idea who each one is. And eventually you will watch most of them run, lose money on some (most) and win a little money on others. Some will become chapters in this book. They will all have a place in six weeks.

They have one thing in common today—high hopes. Each horse walks off the ramp of the Saratoga shuttle carrying a load of plans, dreams and visions. Horse racing, horses for that matter, attract the world's dreamers. Every horse I see stepping down the loading chute this week, to me describable as gray or bay, small or large, filly or colt, is to someone else the wheels of their hope. Whether it's leading trainer Bill Mott or win-one-at-the-meet trainer Anthony Bizelia, horsemen hang Saratoga dreams on their horses every year.

Saratoga and its horses remind me of grade school and its students. When a parent drives to the schoolyard, the other kids are simply other kids. Then your little Katy comes bounding to the car, one child in the world of children. Every horse is someone's Katy.

The vans signify the start is nearly here. You should drive up I-87

The horses are
in town.
(Harlan Marks)

when all you see are giant tractor trailers full of the actors for this
amazing show.

Today, I checked on Succeed (my Katy) first thing. Took him for a
walk, turned him out in a round pen and then a bigger paddock. He
seemed alert and fresh considering his hard day yesterday.

We got the X-rays back on Cinch—nothing's broken. The veteri-
narians think he pulled his suspensory ligament, which in time will
be OK, and maybe he can be someone's riding horse after it heals. I
prayed for that last night.

It still breaks my heart to walk by his stall. He's as uncomfortable
as a blind date. He just looks at you with a faraway look. He's smart
though, and tries to lie down as much as he can. We all wonder why
we can't save all the horses all the time. When I look at Cinch with a

relatively minor injury, as far as threatening his life, I realize how impossible it is to keep a horse off a broken leg. Horses don't speak and you can't tell them to keep their 1,000 pounds off the injured limb.

Imagine going to the hospital in unbearable pain and not being able to talk to the doctor. All you know is that you're in a horrid state. When I'm asked if I have a hero, I point to horses like Cinch—generous creatures that turn off their selfishness and give away their souls.

Cinch makes me sad. He was on the Triple Crown Trail with trainer Carl Nafzger a couple of years ago, now he's faced with mortality. I just keep hoping he'll be a pet one day.

After mourning with Cinch and playing with Succeed, I headed over to my real job, or one of them. I galloped three horses for Leo O'Brien this morning: Jeana Marie, Doc Martin and Fair Jordan.

Pretty easy day at Leo's. We have only 10 horses in right now, so with three riders it was a breeze. We went out in three sets. Galloping horses might be the only thing I've mastered in life. I've been at it forever and it certainly isn't rocket science. It's more fun, like everything, at Saratoga. I like to find a horse or two who can be my projects for the season. Nothing like going to the races to see one of the horses you exercise every day run in a race. You feel like you helped. Whether it's helping a 2-year-old filly win the first at Saratoga or saving a patient in an emergency room or fixing the engine of a broken down Ford, life is sure more interesting and rewarding when you have a role that makes you feel important. Or necessary. Or even just a little helpful. Sometimes the search for that feeling might be all we have.

The first horse who gave me that feeling at Saratoga was Fearless Leader in 1989.

Trainer Mickey Preger and Fearless Leader taught me what to do as a Saratoga exercise rider. Mr. Preger was my first boss outside of my father. His horse was my second.

On my first day, Mr. Preger told me to get on the "Old Horse". Anybody watching could have seen Fearless Leader licking his chops. I was told to gallop once around from wherever he started galloping. Vague instructions until I met the 11-year-old.

The Old Horse and the young jockey went out and raced Kentucky Derby winner Winning Colors every day. When you're as old as Fearless Leader you do whatever you want, whenever you want. The Old Horse would jog until he was ready to gallop and then bust off into flat-out speed while I was still in the jogging seat. Out the back I would go, and out the front Fearless Leader would take me. At least on the straightaways. When you have been going around and around for as many years as he had, you do it your way.

He would canter, in slow speed around the turns and then take off on the straight parts. Fine, except for Winning Colors, who would inevitably be on the track at the same time. We passed each other a good five or six times every day. Me on my old claimer and some poor, pissed off exercise rider on the Billion Dollar Filly.

Fearless Leader was one of those few horses who make a game out of the mundane. That's why he made it to old age. I was just one small piece in his lifelong puzzle. I'm always asked what horses are like. They are just like people. Smart ones, dumb ones, funny ones, generous ones, selfish ones, deliberate ones, sporadic ones, fast ones, slow ones, stubborn ones, honest ones. Fearless Leader was just like an old man who got a kick out of his paper boy, the holly tree in the backyard, the cracking paint in the hallway. Fearless Leader made light of it all. God bless him.

Succeed, Cinch, Amarettitorun, Fearless Leader—all they did was make me feel a part of something.

Mornings will get longer as we get more horses and less help. And less sleep.

This life—I should say lifestyle—is a glorious one. It's like we never really have to step up and face our demons as long as we have the racetrack, the horses, the cushion of it all. But there are no days off and we're at work by 5:30 a.m. every day. Physically, it's a challenge. Mentally, it's a breeze.

Racetrack people are an amazing group. The great American melting pot has no soup like the racetrack.

Today I received instructions from Irishman Leo O'Brien, said hello to New Yorker Orlando Emmolo on the way to the track, waved to Flaco who's from some Spanish-speaking country, passed French-man Christophe Clement's barn and returned Fair Jordan to Ray from Mexico.

Saratoga backside—the World Wide Web.

Off to take a nap now; I need to be rested up for tonight. I'm on a panel at the Racing Museum, a sort of Saratoga kickoff. Jockey Mike Smith, trainer Todd Pletcher and me. Guess who doesn't fit?

TALKING
Tuesday, July 27

"I love the horses. I just come to see the horses. They are so beautiful."

A chatty but very nice woman said this to me as I walked out of the Hall of Fame seminar last night. I wasn't taking notes, not really even thinking about my column. I was, to be honest, standing outside the door of the Hall of Fame waiting for Keith O'Brien while thinking about how I did up there.

On the way to the car, I started thinking about how my new friend felt about horses. I never asked for her name, that's how preoccupied I was with my appraisal of my performance. But I got to thinking about what she said and the way she said it. Maybe that's it, maybe that's the whole reason Saratoga is our Savior.

Horses.

Horses are beautiful. Saratoga is beautiful. Put them together and you have Saratoga in August (I know it starts in July and ends in September but for now on we're going to stick with Saratoga in August), the one time every person can say there is no other place they would rather be. One of the few moments in life where everybody has the same reason for being in the same place. You have a friend in every store, park and bar because we are all here for the same reason. It might range from betting to riding, but the horse is why we're here. It's the one time in my life that I'm doing something people understand and respect. I don't feel alone in my attraction to racing. At home, sometimes I feel like I'm the fool. Here, everyone understands what it's all about.

It feels like an accomplishment every time I arrive in Saratoga, just knowing I survived another year. I've changed in the off-season but I don't really know or care now that I'm in town. I've endured some tragedies in the last year, but Saratoga replenishes the heart. At least for one six-week period, life makes sense. Time will be well spent.

Today is a strange feeling. Empty stalls. Empty houses. Pyramids of boxes shipped in from Belmont Park and all over the world. Ryder. UPS. SUVs packed to the roof.

People respond to the "Ready?" with, "Always ready for this place."

Yes we are.

Even the horses know it's coming. The place is chaotic. Last-minute touches and strategies. The horses realize something is on its way. I don't think they know it's Saratoga per se, but they know the big time has arrived. Horses sense feelings in humans. They react to confidence, stress, nervousness, attitude. The smarter they are, the more they react. They know that we have never acted like this before so something is up. The ones who have been here before, I think, recognize the behavior patterns and react accordingly.

The competitive ones rise to the occasion. The nervous ones find life even harder to endure at Saratoga. This is not a place for the faint of heart, horse or man.

Maybe it's the way we look at them, but they just look different at Saratoga. Succeed could have only looked the way he did on Sunday at Saratoga. He's a proud horse with presence but Saratoga pulls it out of him like a sponge.

Even the mundane looks better at Saratoga.

The chairs are stacked and ready for tomorrow. The picnic tables are stained and await the masses. The squirrels look skinny before their feast—you're not the only one who puts on weight at Saratoga. The grass is green and trimmed. The rails are bright white. The infield lake looks perfect for sailing. The streets are spotless.

The college kids get tutored in how to wait on tables, how to direct traffic and how to lead a horse. Cops get lessons in crowd control and horse sense (they usually fail the latter).

Saratoga 1999 is about 24 hours away. It's like Christmas Eve.

The atmosphere won't start for real until tomorrow. The charm is here now. But the buzz will begin when the people line up on Union Avenue and the horses start the walk from their sanctuarial barns to the lights of the first race.

It's a long season up here so people lay low the day before the meet. It's stretching time today. Adjusting the clocks, fine-tuning the violin for tomorrow's grand opening.

We did our seminar last night. Still not sure how I fit in with Mike Smith and Todd Pletcher, but it was fun and I hoped I provided something useful. They asked me to mention one horse I was looking forward to riding. I had to laugh when I looked out across the auditorium at Keith and Fenneka. They knew it was coming.

"Well, I do a lot of hustling. Planned rides are scarce, but there is one. His name is Succeed and he's the greatest horse that ever lived."

The audience looked intrigued. When I mentioned Mark Hennig and Flawlessly they were seriously intrigued. Some still think steeplechasing uses some other breed of horse. Like there is the Arabian, the Draft Horse, the Thoroughbred and the Steeplechaser. The same breed, my friends. Jerry Bailey rode Succeed before he became a jumper.

Mike Smith is a natural public speaker. Quick-witted and insightful, Mike had everybody laughing and understanding horse racing a little better than when they walked in.

Mike mentioned trying to get back to the same level as last year. I talk about being tested at Saratoga—Mike had had the SATs, LSATs, and the GREs thrown at him in one punch last year.

On his way to being leading jockey at the meet, he was on a different level. And then Dacron went flying into the inside hedge of the turf course and Mike catapulted through the air. He went from being leading jockey at Saratoga to another patient in an Albany hospital. I'll never forget that moment.

I was watching the race with Mike's wife Patrice, over by the jocks' room. Actually we were sitting with our backs to the TV, talking, when we heard that shudder thud from the crowd. If you've been around the track, you know the noise the crowd makes when there is a fall. It's unmistakable. Indescribable. Sickening.

We knew when we heard the sound—I just knew it was Mike. We took off running to the track, Patrice screaming, "Who was it?" But we knew. I remember just running, trying to keep up with Patrice and praying for Mike as I ran. He broke two vertebrae. I remember seeing him leaning on the outside rail, watching all the other jockeys pulling up, trying to see good signs in the melee that had occurred.

Mike looked at me and handed me the two black rubber bands that keep his silks taut around his wrists (a Roy Hobbs move). Mike said he'd be OK. I still have the rubber bands, and I'll use them on Thursday.

Mike Smith looking
for a big meet.
(Barbara D. Livingston)

Mike was out forever trying to rehab his back. Now he's in Saratoga again. He said last night that he wanted to get back to the feeling of last year, when something special was happening.

That was part of the impetus to start the book, to tell about guys like Mike who go through moments like this. They happen every day at Saratoga. Last night they showed the Hopeful, when Lucky Roberto and Robbie Davis won the best 2-year-old stakes of the summer. Mike was supposed to ride the horse. I looked at Mike when the tape was over and I said, "You all right?" He tried to wipe the 'what could have been' look off his face and attempted to smile. "About that time, I was trying to get a coat hanger down my cast to scratch my back," he said.

Chip and I visited Mike in the hospital and watched him try to adjust to his shackle. He looked pathetic. When they say body cast, they mean body cast. He was wrapped like a mummy from neck to waist in white plaster.

Here was our friend who lifted weights in the sauna with us every Wednesday and Thursday (he doing the lifting) and awed us every day with rides from heaven, lying in a hospital bed trying to use the bathroom with dignity.

Two young girls came in to visit him, and looked at a gimpy man wrapped in plaster.

Mike just smiled. "Don't be scared girls, horses are good."

They smiled anyway.

So there's one person you can cheer for at Saratoga. The place owes him one.

Now, more about Saratoga. Think culture, history, pizzazz, color, energy. You name it, Saratoga has it. Old and young at the same time, the impossible combination. Old trees. Old buildings. Old tales. New life. New dreams. New sensations.

Every day during the racing season is a new life. Each day lives by itself, with choices, opportunities and once-in-a-lifetime moments. I'm sure life everywhere has these, but you have to look for them. At Saratoga, they bombard you. At Saratoga, your eyes widen without even knowing it.

The racetrack is the hub. The oldest racetrack in the country stands halfway down Union Avenue, like a shepherd over his flock. Racing at Saratoga proves that all good things are not gone. That tradition matters. That the human race does recognize the essence when its there for them.

But my mind wanders to the old days (and I'm not that old). I still miss the old pony track that ran through the trees on the Oklahoma side. They made it a road. Damn asphalt right over Collin's hoofprints.

It's never good when grass and sand become concrete and asphalt. Bums me out every time I think of "expansion." I'm still not too keen on the winner's circle; there's something about the old chalk line that I miss. I'll think of some more things that have changed and are never coming back. I try to look at the good of what is here and hope that some progressive thinker doesn't tinker with greatness.

Tomorrow is opening day. At last.

DING DING DING

Wednesday, July 28

As the bell tolls.

The turnstiles are spinning. I just dropped some tack off at the jocks' room and walked into the eye of Saratoga.

Remember the vibrating football game? You would set your team up against your buddy's. Everything would be in perfect formation and order. And then you would flip the switch.

Opening Day 1999, the lines are out to Union Avenue. The dreams reach the moon. All the world is young.

It starts early. Picnic tables were snatched up at daybreak. There's nothing like riding the second set of the day and seeing people pouring mimosas, kids eating Cheerios and adults drinking beer. Saratoga is back.

I'm late already. I need to get over and see the first, a steeplechase, and, no, I'm not riding; I'll get over it one day. My agent skills let me down for today's race. I had four maybe rides, which in a span of 10 minutes became four somebody else's rides.

Too busy to worry.

Remember when I said it's like Christmas Eve? The kids are about to get up and Santa Claus still hasn't reached the chimney. This morning was wild.

First thing I walked into was a loose horse. I turned the corner of the Annex to see how Succeed was doing out in his paddock and a runaway horse gave me a good-morning brush. He was much more interested in another horse and left me alone. It was a scene, one colt, one filly, a hundred fools trying to prod someone to do something. The couple ran into one empty stall and before anybody could get to the door, they were out again.

Dad told me a long time ago, "Sean, when you see something like this . . . don't get involved." Old-time horsemen will save your life, if you listen.

So today I avoided the ruckus and bolted to Succeed, who was front and center for the show (he gave it three stars), until they finally got the two horses back in one stall with the door latched. Welcome to Saratoga. They were just a few of the loose ones this morning. I told you the horses know something is up.

Part of it is pure science. The mornings are sprightly up here. Most of these horses had been waking up in the stale, humid, polluted air of Belmont Park. Today, they awoke to light, chilly, country air which makes them all feel better. Horses tend to get loose when they feel the cool air.

Two horses that weren't loose today will be worth watching tomorrow. Grenade and More Than Ready. They are the direct opposites, except that they'll probably both be favored and they both are as talented as they get.

Grenade is a 10-year-old jumper, giant in stature, actual height and class. More Than Ready is a 2-year-old who might just tip over the world. One's on his way out and the other is already on his way up. They both have hearts of dynamite.

Take a look at Grenade, in the paddock and in the *Daily Racing Form,* and you'll see why I'm writing about him. He's a giant horse.

Grenade in full. *(Barbara D. Livingston)*

Black as night. And so cool. He looks like Zorro. And he comes to Saratoga every year with his sword drawn. He made three starts in 1998, including a 2-for-2 mark at the Spa. The year before he ran four times, won once at Saratoga. In 1996, he made five starts, with one win at Saratoga. The horse loves it here.

"He knows where he is," said his jockey, Chip Miller. "How could he not?"

I checked on him this morning. He's like the badass of steeple-chasing.

I also found More Than Ready. Now remove yourself from Grenade's image. More Than Ready was standing in the middle of his stall with his head about eye level in the straw. He looked at me, noticed I had nothing to offer except a notepad and pen, and kept his head buried in his bedding. He picked his head up as a horse walked past his window in the back and again when a horse stepped onto the pavement in front of him. He seemed ultra-intelligent and a little kidlike, too. Good horses seem to be aware of everything around them. They have a sense of place and worth.

Trainer Todd Pletcher told me about him: "He's smart, one of those laid-back types who does whatever you ask. He has a lot of personality. He sticks his tongue out and always wants attention. He's one of those horses who has a little presence. He'll walk around here knowing that he's one of the stars."

Tomorrow he is the star. The horse looks like a lock in the Sanford, the first stakes for male 2-year-olds at Saratoga. Undefeated in four starts, with a track record, More Than Ready has never even been tested.

"Every time he's hit the wire, in his works and his races, he's had something left. That's a good sign. He's been special so far, we'll just try to keep him healthy and happy, we know he has the ability," Pletcher said.

The trainer led the meet last year and likes what he sees this time around.

"We're holding the strongest hand we've ever held in the 2-year-old races," Pletcher said, alluding to More Than Ready tomorrow and his filly Circle of Life in today's Schuylerville Stakes. "To say we're going to come here and win 20 races and the title . . . last year everything came together, just one of those meets when everything went the right way. When we needed a race to fill it filled, when we needed a fast track we got a fast track. Last year we caught them by surprise a little bit, this year we're expected to do well, we're under a microscope, so personally it's a different feel."

Pletcher runs six today and four tomorrow so we'll know right quick what's under the microscope.

FAT THURSDAY
Thursday, July 29—10:10 a.m.

This is going to be quick. I just made a mad dash from Runs Numbers' saddle to my makeshift office. Supposed to be back at the track in 20 minutes to be on Mary Ryan's TV show and then to the sweat box. I just wanted to jump on here and let you know I'm here, safe and sound, but a little wrung out.

I ride Welcome Parade in the first and I'm fat; coming to Saratoga

Chuck Simon, before he became a Saratoga winning trainer. *(Harlan Marks)*

fat is like getting on the boat seasick. Not going to be pretty. I'm not too bad for today, only doing 149, but still need to visit the bane of my Saratoga existence, the sauna.

WELCOME ABOARD

Thursday, July 29—8 p.m.

I have called Saratoga every name in the book. Magical, beautiful, historical, lively, invigorating, inspirational, intimidating. Today it's just been hectic. That's all. Just a long, busy day that I've pretty much screwed up from start to finish. Ever have one of those days when you would have been better off if you stayed in bed? From the time you brushed your teeth the day was on the other team. But I do have a couple of stories to tell, so here goes.

Oh wait, did you see Grenade and More Than Ready? Told you.

The Knight Sky won the seventh race.

As the flashy chestnut went three clear past the wire, I wondered about his connections. I knew the jockey, Robby Albarado, who rode here last year and does well wherever he goes—but the trainer, Chuck Simon? Look down the race's program, typical headline conditioners Stanley Hough, Todd Pletcher, Rusty Arnold, Mike Hushion . . . and Chuck Simon. Sounds like a shortstop for the Texas Rangers.

I walked down to the winner's circle to see who this Chuck Simon character really is.

And found out I know Chuck Simon. He's Allen Jerkens' assistant trainer. He's the tall guy with the shaved head on the right side of Kelly Kip and Wagon Limit and all Jerkens' horses. I've seen him for years, never spoken to him; intimidating fellow, really. Like most of the world, until you meet him.

I followed Albarado through the crowd after the race—he split (why's he in such a hurry after the race?)—and here's Chuck Simon and his people. Orlando the exercise rider gives him a slap. "My man Chuck, put it to 'em." Dave the hotwalker congratulates him. Carlos, who walks hots for John Hertler and checks hand stamps grabs his hand in one of those half the arm shakes.

Not a tie in sight, not a boxholder to be found—this was one of the little people gone big. This was the bat boy swinging for the fences. Chuck Simon just smiled like he didn't know what happened.

Chuck, you just won your first race at Saratoga on opening day. You're the local boy who came home to win with a 35-1 shot over a Dogwood Stable/Pletcher chalk. Chuck, you just made The Chief so proud. The Chief is H. Allen Jerkens, the Giant Killer, Hall of Famer and the ethereal presence on the New York backstretch.

"I'm relieved. You look at the *Racing Form* and see every big trainer, every big jockey, and every big horse; it's a little intimidating," said the 32-year-old Simon, who went out on his own in May when Ken and Sarah Ramsey gave him a stable full of horses. "Now you make the decisions instead of the suggestions. This was a good decision."

The Knight Sky was making his turf debut. Simon made that deci-

sign and accounting for the horse's sire, Sky Classic, favorite in the 1992 Breeders' Cup Turf. That's what trainers are paid to do, like stockbrokers. They need to produce for their clients using knowledge and intuition. They make their living on commission, but have to put up their own capital most of the time. After watching The Knight Sky cover the grass, you could see it was a perfect decision with plenty of commission in the future.

Simon, who went to high school in Saratoga and lived in Ballston Lake, looked off in disbelief as he was interviewed. Another one of his people gave him a high five and a giant smile. I asked Simon who that guy was, and he just said, "Oh he works in the spit box." The spit box is racetrack slang for the test barn, where the horses go to be tested for illegal substances. That's where Simon would go with Jerkens' horse. That's where assistant trainers go. Simon's assistant trainer is on his way there with The Knight Sky. Simon made that trek with The Chief's horses for four years—and loved every step.

"It's the best assistant trainer job in the world. I got the job by telling him he needed me. He asked me why I wanted to work for

The Chief and his horse. *(Barbara D. Livingston)*

him (and not for a more glitzy operation like a Pletcher, Nick Zito, or D. Wayne Lukas). I told him I wanted to be a horse trainer, not a movie star. He liked that," Simon laughed. "He treats you like a man. He wants you to learn on your own. Watch him and you will learn. He told me you have got to know what's wrong with a horse before everyone, before the vet. . . . You know how much they eat. Where they stand in the stall. How they travel."

Jerkens is a legend around the racetrack. He is known for his work ethic, absolute will to succeed, and his attention to detail. Not the prettiest shedrow on the grounds, but his horses come first. Jerkens is called the Giant Killer for pulling upsets on the racetrack. He's the one who beat Secretariat with jokers named Onion and Prove Out. And Kelso three times with Beau Purple. More recently it was Skip Away with Wagon Limit.

Simon couldn't say enough about Jerkens and, in so doing, about horsemanship.

"One trait I inherited from him is being self-critical, just trying to do the right thing all the time, sometimes you'll overdo it," Simon said. "He told me when I left: Use your head. Do what you think is right. And pay attention to the horse."

As soon as the interview was over, Simon was on his way to the barn he used to call home to see his old boss.

I almost asked if I could tag along but it felt wrong, like it might take something away from the moment; this was their day. But I'd kill to be a squirrel in a tree.

"He'll be as happy as I am. He treats me like one of his sons. He'll still make little suggestions . . . 'You might want to try . . .' "

Simon continued to gush.

"He's 40 years older than me and I can't keep up with the man, he never rests," Simon said. "He's one of those guys who cares so much it will drive him crazy. He's a once in a lifetime guy."

The way Simon talks and the way The Knight Sky ran, there might be two of them.

AND AWAY WE GO
Friday, July 30

I woke up this morning realizing how much The Knight Sky and Chuck Simon meant to me and this book. I'm on it now. This whole book/daily column gig had me a little overwhelmed; can you be a little overwhelmed? I just was fighting it a little. I don't know why, but I just wasn't clicking with this whole assignment until yesterday.

I had to fight the urge to stay on my conservative ass when The Knight Sky won. When I left my friends in the box after the race to find out who in the hell Chuck Simon was, this journal had its breakthrough. We're on our way. My editor asked me a day or two ago if I was going to talk to anyone, like interview people? Well Kevin, now I am.

For some reason, I hesitate when it comes to walking up and talking to people. When I do, I'm glad I did, and all is well. Thanks, Chuck.

Now how about today?

I wandered over to the picnic area between Union Avenue and the paddock. This is where families plop down for a day at the races. The horses walk between two white plastic fences from their barns, which are on the other side of Union Avenue. That's the two-lanes-each-way road that pretty much serves as the main vein in Saratoga. If you don't know where Union Avenue is or haven't experienced some bump in your pulse there, then you haven't been to Saratoga.

The road runs long and straight. It takes you to Saratoga Lake in one direction and to downtown Saratoga in the other.

The horses walk right across Union to get from Horse Haven to the main track. Traffic stops as the horses go to work. It's a cool spot to see a horse walk to the paddock—and an even better place to see THE horse walk to the paddock.

"What number is that?" asked the fan leaning on the horse-path rail that connects the stable area to the paddock.

More Than Ready
is just that.
(Barbara D. Livingston)

"More Than Ready," came the response. No number, just More Than Ready.

"Hey, that's the one, hey, there he is," said the now upright and alert fan beckoning to his picnic-blanket comrades to get up and see The One. They missed him—too much beer to keep from spilling and chicken to keep from tipping.

Nonetheless, He is The One. More Than Ready is the best 2-year-old in the country. He's undefeated and on his way to fame and fortune. In Thoroughbred racing, the 2-year-olds are the freshmen. The ones who replenish the hope. Saratoga is Harvard. MIT. Yale. The 2-year-olds here are the best in the country. Give it a rest California. More Than Ready is the best 2-year-old at Saratoga. And here he is.

More Than Ready appeared from the barn area at 4:55, along with six Todd Pletcher employees. One on the shank, one leading the charge, two at the flanks and two at the rear. All you needed was a "Forward, March" order and guns across the shoulders.

A set of white rundown bandages on his hind legs, a bright white shadow roll, white bridle, long leather reins with black rubber, a loose D-bit in his mouth, leather-covered shank under his gum, ears straight ahead, braided forelock, killer walk, great shake. Cool, calm, inquisitive—like he knew he hadn't been here before. Harvard would never be the same.

A kid ran up behind him, the horse jigged a step and turned his head to see who would do such a thing. A slow, mission walk. Pletcher made seven as the horse neared the paddock.

More Than Ready just walked around like the exercise at hand was merely an afternoon activity. His nostrils flared as he checked out the Saratoga paddock. Mighty, a beautiful colt trained by Frankie Brothers, whinnied once and More Than Ready answered. Even the whinny sounded secure.

Valets, who help saddle the horses, came out from the jocks' room. More Than Ready stood under the number four tree, professional and patient. Jockey John Velazquez walked out with 13 minutes to post, shook five hands and talked to Pletcher. The jockey and the trainer had an obligatory strategy conversation. Riders up with 11 minutes to post. He galloped to the start by himself and jogged around while the others walked with their ponies. Then they loaded into the gate. And the rest was a mockery.

More Than Ready won the Sanford by almost 10 lengths yesterday. The undefeated colt was a sight. He demolished a solid group of 2-year-olds. The son of Southern Halo broke sharply but was still outbroken by second-choice Dance Master. Inside the quick Dance Master around the turn; it almost looked like it might be in doubt. Velazquez switched lanes and More Than Ready flew home. You should have seen him come down the lane. This is one you can say that you saw. You were there.

Pletcher said a couple of days ago that More Than Ready always finishes with something left. Amen to that. The horse looked like he was using about 50 percent and could have gone around a couple more times. This was an awesome performance.

Whenever someone mentions Saratoga highlights, More Than Ready will be right up there with all the one-day legends.

He's a great looking colt and all I can think is please stay sound and give us our hero. Racing fans try not to get too excited about one precious horse. It seems they are all so fleeting. I can't help but take a bittersweet approach when I see a horse like More Than Ready. We have all been here before, in awe of a brilliant horse, only to see that horse fall away to injury or mismanagement. Horse gone, dream gone. Imagine seeing one and only one John Elway fourth-quarter comeback or half a season of Mark McGwire and Sammy Sosa. That happens all the time in racing.

For my part, I was anything but heroic yesterday. I finished third on Welcome Parade, nosed out in a four-way photo finish for second. Grenade did his Saratoga thing—winning easily in his first start since October.

My horse ran well given his trip from hell. I need to apologize to a couple of people who wanted to talk to me after the race. I usually avoid any contact when I get in a huff like I did yesterday, because the only impression I'm going to make is a bad one. I told my best friend Chip Miller exactly what I thought about his ride on Grenade when we pulled up. Chip managed to bull his way through Welcome Parade with a circuit to go. And I was still kicking and screaming on my way back to the jocks' room. Only thing I could do was go home and write a story. Guess who's spending the night in my house? I'll get over it and be friends with Chip soon, but right now I'm about ready to throw his clothes in the street.

As for my friend Patty Jones: I'm sorry for not stopping on my way through the grandstand. I knew the impression I was going to make was far from favorable. I wanted to stop and finally meet you after all of our e-mails. Blame Chip. Nah, you can blame me, but immediately separating myself from a heated four-minute race will forever be an unmasterable task. Golf, women, ballroom dancing and that. I know I'm supposed to be a good sport and leave the racetrack behind, and I'm better now than ever before, but I could not stop and talk after Welcome Parade got Grenaded halfway through his race.

I had to keep walking. Hope you understood.

SHOWING OFF
Saturday, July 31

A day at Saratoga is part vacation, part work. Did I write that? Can't seem to find the vacation yet this year. Saratoga 1999 is out of control at the moment. I have four jobs and try to balance them all each day.

This year, I decided I didn't want idle time, that space of relaxation that sends me into overthinking—the time of the day when I know I'm wasting what's inside me. The time when I eat too much, lay around too much, nap, or just wander without purpose. The "What the hell, I'll have a beer, got nothing else to do" time. I'll give you one of those "I have a friend" lines. I have friends who head to the Parting Glass after they finish working at the barn at noon. I know I'll spend enough time in the Glass to have them hand me an Anchor Steam when I walk in the door, but at least this year I'll feel like I deserve it. Maybe. All I know is I wanted to accomplish something this year. I just wanted to fix that time of nothing. So I corrected it the best way I could. This book is what I have to show for it.

Now, there's no time to plummet into depression or overthink everything. If I stay busy, I avoid those times. I still overthink, get depressed, but now there is no time to dwell so I come out of them quicker. Or something like that.

Still working on the digital camera, that's a column in itself, so you'll have some art to go along with all these words. Still trying to find a tailor so I'll have an extra suit and a new sport coat to wear before the meet ends. Working on Succeed, rode him for the last two day; he was all horse today. Took him to the track for the first time since his race. He liked the action and told me those four days off made him crazy. Nah, he's not crazy but whew, was he feeling good. Glad to have him moving and feeling so chippy after his first steeplechase. Hopefully, he'll run here in three or four weeks. You'll know all about it, for better or worse.

Remember Cinch? The X-rays showed nothing and the scans

showed nothing, so he's not nearly as bad as we thought. Still not sure of the plans for the rest of his life, but at least they are optimistic. He seems better in the stall, moving around with a little more freedom. He looks like he has accepted his state. I wish we could tell him he will get better, that he will eventually be free again. Instead, we take care of him the best we can. Oats, water, hay, medicine and poultice (a claylike substance designed to reduce heat and swelling in his legs), but we are unable to soothe his worry over the way he feels.

I still hope he finds some young kid wanting a horse that looks like Secretariat.

Speaking of which (am I good with these transitions to Succeed or what?). . . .

I took Succeed to see Cindy Hutter, assistant to Todd Pletcher. I've known Cindy since she was working for Chip's dad back when all we rode were ponies. She is a friend I see at Saratoga every year. We have a morning-on-the-backside relationship, I show her a horse like Succeed and she shows me a horse like Rare Rock.

A couple of years ago, she rode Rare Rock past our barn. I was cleaning tack and looked at this incredible creature she was riding. I asked her, "Who's that?" She looked at me with pure disdain and said "Rare Rock." Like, "How dare you ask?" Not in a bad way—she just was taking great pride in her big horse and assumed the whole world thought of him like she did.

Today, I rode up on Succeed and said, "Cindy, this is my Rare Rock." She knew what I meant. She walked over, gave him a big pat and marveled at the sight of him. He's like a beautiful date. Say, look at me and what's around my arm.

Cindy's date flexed his muscles yesterday.

Rare Rock made his first start yesterday since last year's Breeders' Cup. The 6-year-old has presence. A horse who stands out. With Pat Day perched up on his long neck, Rare Rock won a $52,000 allowance race. I asked Pat how much fun he is to ride. To me he looks like the ultimate in joyrides. Big, long, free-running horse who tries every time.

"Ahh, he's great fun. He's a real willing participant. Likes to run up against the bit. Got good speed and puts you in the race and you're along for the ride," Day said.

Now that sounds like fun. To be Pat Day.

Or Chris McCarron.

McCarron came to Saratoga to ride the favorite in the Test Stakes on Saturday. He left with three fewer pairs of goggles, a cracked voice and a sore writing hand. He finished up the track on Olympic Charmer. She might not have liked the heat, maybe the ship from California. She definitely didn't like the dirt in her face, according to McCarron, who also shipped in from the West Coast.

"It wasn't her day and I don't know why," McCarron said to a slew of reporters after the race won by the Pletcher-trained Marley Vale. McCarron has to rank at the top of any list of jockeys to interview in the sport. He takes his time, gives you well-thought-out answers and articulates the point.

Watching him move through the Saratoga crowd after traveling across the country and losing on the favorite was inspiring. McCar-

Chris McCarron stops
and takes the time.
(Barbara D. Livingston)

ron would have stopped to talk to Patty Jones. He would have kissed her hello, met her family, redecorated her dining room, if she asked. She would have been thrilled and now that I'm thinking about it, that's more important than winning or losing a race any day. I'm writing "Be more like Chris" on my calendar as we speak.

McCarron shook hands with old friends, introduced reporters, signed programs, photos and even one beer can cozy. McCarron is one of those people I like to watch. I like the thought he puts into his job, his life. The perfect question: Chris, what is Saratoga like?

"Saratoga is class. Excitement. History," McCarron said. "A lot of history in Thoroughbred racing is traced to the beautiful spa in upstate New York."

See what I mean about articulating?

The second question. Did you ever think about riding here during the meet?

"Yes," quipped the Massachusetts native, "during the meet, but never when the meet wasn't running."

He's got a great sense of humor, too.

"I always wanted to ride here but never gave it any serious consideration because, I think, I never had enough confidence in myself to relinquish my business at home and go back and try to recover it. And uprooting the family," McCarron said. "I wonder what it would have been like. I wish I had ridden here for the whole meet. Now maybe I have the time to think about it. Maybe I will end up here one of these summers."

There's a scoop. Can you imagine having Chris McCarron to factor into your handicapping formulas? Have McCarron ride every day next to Jerry Bailey, Pat Day, John Velazquez, Mike Smith, Jorge Chavez, Shane Sellers. Now that would be fun. Invite Kent Desormeaux, Frankie Dettori, and Laffit Pincay, too.

So yes, that's what we're doing. At Saratoga and dreaming about how it could be better. See why I shouldn't have idle time?

ONE INCH

Sunday, August 1

Get up. Walk across the room. One foot in front of the other. Look down at your feet. Right foot wins. Left foot wins. Right foot wins. Left foot wins. Right foot. Left foot.

Victory Gallop and Behrens won and lost the Whitney this way. The last desperate strides, Behrens wins. Victory Gallop wins. Behrens wins. Victory Gallop wins. Behrens. Victory Gallop.

When the wire finally decided the foot, it was Victory Gallop whose nose came down while Behrens' nose came up on a $220,000 bob of the head. That was also the difference in the rights to number one and maybe the Eclipse Award by the end of the year. The first Saratoga hero of 1999.

Billed as the race of the year, the 1999 Whitney certainly proved to be the race of the meet. Behrens settled about midpack while Vic-

Victory Gallop and Behrens. *(Barbara D. Livingston)*

tory Gallop was back with the ambulance. It was one of those races where you can't watch both horses at the same time. I played binocular tennis. Check on Behrens: cruising, outside, should be smooth trip from there. Victory Gallop; way back but comfortable, in his style, only one horse beaten and that's longshot Catienus.

On the far turn, I needed only one eye. Jorge Chavez sent Behrens four wide and Victory Gallop made an explosive move that in an instant made me think "race of the year." Jerry Bailey's white cap was just blowing past the field. The kick was astonishing—one of those moves that is so fast the crowd doesn't even really see it until it's halfway over. The place went crazy. At the head of the stretch, Behrens was on the inside and Victory Gallop on the outside. This is why people pay the salary-rents up here, why they sweat in suits at the races all day. This is why people come to Saratoga.

It was Victory Gallop trying to catch Coronado's Quest in last year's Travers. It was Behrens trying to hold off Deputy Commander in the 1997 Travers. They both lost those classics by a head-bob. Maybe they knew that as they came down the lane. They looked like they had something to prove. This was a Saratoga horse race.

Victory Gallop put his head in front, and he looked like the winner in a good race. If it ended just like that, there would not be a complaint on the grounds. Then Behrens did what we revere in the Thoroughbred: he fought back. The crowd knew it, Bailey knew it, he knew it. The last jumps to the wire, it was the head-bob. One stride you win, the next you lose.

Talk about a race no one deserved to lose. They crossed the wire and no one knew. People just slumped in their chairs knowing they watched the best the sport can give, the best the horse can provide. I had chills. My program was on the floor, my coat, too. I can't remember who I bet, who I was rooting for. Someone asked the time of the race. I had no idea. Someone asked who was third, and I looked at them with an "Oh yeah, there were other horses."

The numbers went up and the 1A rose to the top. Victory Gallop was on the right stride. Behrens the wrong. They came back to an ovation. First Behrens, then Victory Gallop.

James Bond, trainer of Behrens, and Denny McCabe, Jorge

Chavez's valet and friend, just stood together and alone in the middle of the track. Sullen. Then the crowd cheered. They slowly started clapping and began to move. Like they knew this was the game, the highest of highs and lowest of lows. They patted their horse and then applauded Victory Gallop when he returned to the cameras and cheering section. Bailey pumped his fist a couple of times, more emotion than he usually shows. Trainer Elliott Walden tried to engineer the process of getting the horse cool and getting him and the rest of the team into the winner's circle. Owners Jack and Art Preston kept saying, "I wish he wouldn't make it so close all the time."

We don't. These are the races that keep us coming back. Victory Gallop, we owe you big. Behrens, too.

The reporters and photographers swarmed Walden and Bailey after the ceremony. Victory Gallop and Behrens headed to the test barn, still with a little bounce in their steps. The crowd that painted the apron with hats a minute ago retreated to the shade of the grandstand. Behrens was a long way in front of Victory Gallop this time—he didn't have his picture taken. Victory Gallop, his groom and his exercise rider took their time up the stretch. Them petting him and him slowing his bounce to a collected walk.

Back at the test barn, where they would give a urine sample to check for prohibited substances, Behrens and Victory Gallop tried to cool down. They swapped bridles for halters and walked around the short barn trying to get the wobble out of their legs, the beat back in their hearts, the air back in their lungs. Behrens dove for his water bucket, stuck his whole head in the cold water. About 10 gulps. The chain shank around his nose became taut and he was hauled out of the water.

Victory Gallop actually looks more tired than Behrens. He's coughing like a cancer patient. Sounds like a dirt cough, the horse inhaled half the track. He's the same way at his bucket. He walks and coughs. The two providers now walk around the barn, five feet apart. They get ice bandages on their front legs, are hosed off, then bathed with soap. With each turn, the nostrils slow down and the pressured looks release. The horses now realize they will catch their breath, they will again feel their legs.

Their friends and coworkers won't. Mark Shuman and Maxine Owen, assistant trainer and exercise rider for Behrens, retreat to the shade. Shuman can barely speak. His shirt sleeves are rolled above his elbows, sweat still stains his forehead. Owen—she might cry with one wrong word. These people awake in the four hour every day to see that these horses eat enough, drink enough, train enough, walk enough. Then they go out and watch their project, their friend—and themselves—lose by an inch.

"I can't believe it, a dirty rotten nose," Owen said to nobody. "Why'd they give us one earlier?" The Bond stable won a photo in the fifth with Bestbandintheland.

Behrens and Victory Gallop slowly caught their breath, the last race went running past, dirty blinkers sat in a bucket and the Bond crew tried to get their senses back. They weren't sulking, just clenching their teeth and wishing for an inch.

"I think I might be sick. Feels like we need a year off after that," Shuman says. "I'll never watch the replay."

A sentence later, he switched to the positive side. "The only thing is [Behrens] thinks he won and he can't lose his confidence after that."

Behrens didn't look like a loser as he walked around the test barn. Neither did Victory Gallop. Wonder if they know? Seems like they might. That's the mystery of horses.

On the winning side, Shannon Ritter, who gallops Victory Gallop, came over and talked to the Bond team, a "we're-all-in-this-together" conversation. Ritter has lost photos and won photos, too.

"He's the best horse I've ever been around. He does everything right. He just loves his life," Ritter said. "When Jerry got back I said, 'Way to wait'—the longer you wait the better the kick he has. I'm proud of him. He's a real fun-loving horse, the happiest horse I've ever been around. I thought he won, I thought it was the Belmont when he had his head down." Victory Gallop won the 1998 Belmont over Real Quiet in the same fashion.

Ritter, Owen and Shuman know it was just an inch, but also know they'll get up tomorrow and so will their horses. The 1999 Whitney was horse racing at its best.

Shuman unwrapped the Vetrap from Behrens' hind legs, tie tucked in his shirt, covered in dust and sweat. He rolled the white elastic bandages in a ball, put up a 20-foot jumper at the trash can on the corner of the test barn. The bandageball bounced off the rim. Shuman shook his head. "Just like today."

PARTNERS

Monday, August 2

Damn, I'm exhausted after the Whitney. My friend Chip, and yes, we are friends again, told me long ago, "Write every article like it's the only thing a person will ever read of yours." OK, go read yesterday again.

No, there's more to the wonderful Whitney story.

Every veterinarian has said at least once, "This job would be easy if horses could talk." They don't talk; their efforts speak for them and so do their jockeys, trainers, grooms, exercise riders and anyone

Shannon Ritter and Victory Gallop.
(Barbara D. Livingston)

else who comes to know them. Here's Victory Gallop by way of Shannon Ritter as she followed the Whitney winner back to his barn.

"He did good. I'm proud of him. He's awesome to be around."

"Way to go girl," shouts a fan from a car as Ritter walks and thinks about the day. She smiles and nods at the shared experience. Today is Ritter's day and tomorrow could be for the voice in that car.

"He just does his business. He's always happy. If you were around him, he sticks his tongue out and plays with you. He gets hay in his mouth, shakes his head around. He's a real character."

Ritter, who has worked for Elliott Walden for 2½ years, is the one person on the grounds who knows what Jerry Bailey felt around the far turn.

"The kick is great to feel. He's very smooth. He works like he runs, he wants to relax for the first part and when you ask him to run his afterburners just come on."

I asked Ritter if she ever talks to Bailey about the horse.

"Not too much. I talk to Elliott, and Elliott talks to Jerry."

People like Ritter provide an integral link to the success of horse racing. They ride these horses in the dark, hold the afterburners in check day after day. Stimulation, consolation, education lie delicately within the Ritters of the backstretch. The good relationship is a perfect synthesis between horse and person. Ritter is Victory Gallop's companion and coach. Victory Gallop is Ritter's pride and joy.

"He takes everything into stride. The traveling to Dubai, stabling here, he takes it all in and goes with it. He's really good at it. I thought he won, I thought he had his head bobbing down at the wire, but I wasn't positive."

The tractors rumble past as we walk along the road across from the half-mile pole.

"If you were to get on him in the morning you would see how game he is. I'll be galloping around and he'll see a horse in front of him and he'll have to catch them. Once he gets by them he's happy but he has to get by that other horse."

I think about the fury that I witnessed when he set his sights on Behrens. I can see Ritter feeling the same vision.

"He can be hard to gallop but when it's quiet on the track, it's easy. When he has something to focus on, then he'll take more hold."

Again I think of Behrens, and Victory Gallop seeing him as a dead duck in the stretch.

A horn blows at Ritter. "Thanks Doc."

"When we work him, we'll give a horse a head start of 10 lengths and he'll just explode when I ask him to catch up."

We turned the corner of the barn and Victory Gallop was posing again.

"Look at him now. He's proud of himself. He's a big showoff. He loves the camera. He's the best horse I've ever ridden."

Who's the second best?

"Well, I have a personal favorite—he's not the best but one when I used to ride races. Natural Dad. He was just a cheap horse at Portland Meadows [in Oregon]. I won eight races in one meet on him. He had the track record at Portland Meadows. I rode for eight years, was leading rider at Portland in like '91."

Do you miss it?

"I miss the horses; the people part I don't."

Ritter reflected on her days as a jockey when Victory Gallop walked past, jolting her back to today at Saratoga.

"I was a little more nervous for this one, not sure why. We have a long way to go yet, but he's on top right now and hopefully we'll stay here."

Does he recognize you?

"Well, it's funny you say that. I was watching him earlier today while he was in ice boots and I left for a little while. When I came back the girl who was standing there said to me, 'You know, that horse noticed when you left, he got a little fidgety.' If she didn't say that I probably would have said no. But I guess he does because when I walk up to him, he'll stick his tongue out at me. When Elliott walks up to him, he tries to bite him."

What would you call him? A friend, a coworker, a brother, a what?

"The horse? My kid. He's like my kid."

Did you think I was asking about Elliott?

"I just wanted to make sure."

So you're proud of your kid?

"Yeah."

Can you compare him to another horse?

"I'm galloping Menifee as well. They are totally different. Menifee is like a big brute. He's professional but he needs to go with the pony to backtrack. He'll throw you on the ground if he wanted to. He's more of a horse and Victory's more of a happy-go-lucky, I-don't-care kind of guy. We call Menifee Mike Tyson because he's bulky, looks and acts like a boxer. If you go up to him, he'll want to bite you, where Victory will want to play. But I am very partial to Victory."

SWINGING FOR THE FENCES

Tuesday, August 3

Someone asked me if I had trouble finding material; it's not material, it's time. The racetrack is all material. Stories are everywhere. Life, for that matter, is all material, all stories. Finding the time to tell them remains the challenge.

I will arise tomorrow morning at 5:00, be on Succeed at 5:30, at Leo's by 6:30, back at the Oklahoma Annex by 8:30 for a couple more gallops, then to the jocks' room by 10:00. The sauna by 10:15 (hell by 11:00), out of the sweatbox by noon. On the scale by 12:30 and on top of Inca Colony by 12:50. Careening toward the first by 1:01. Hope to God, in the winner's circle by 1:10. So when do I write in all that mess? The night before.

I told a writer the other day that riding jump races at Saratoga is like having 12 at-bats in Yankee Stadium. If you strike out in all of them, it doesn't matter how many home runs you hit in the parking lot before or after; you're a failure. That's what Saratoga is for me. We have 12 chances to win a race here. Two down already.

We ride from March to November. I rode 101 races last year, won 23, and only one at Saratoga. A bad year can be salvaged by saying, "I won one at Saratoga." It took me seven years to win my first Saratoga race, so I think you can reasonably say that all jump jockeys want to win here more than anywhere else in the world. We get two chances a week at Saratoga. For jump jockeys, Wednesday and Thursday are the axis of our week. Everything centers around what comes down to eight minutes (two races that last about four minutes apiece) in the middle of the week. Win one race and it's your week. Lose both and it's another week of frustration.

Our alter-egos, the flat riders, get nine chances six days a week to win at Saratoga. We constantly defend our frustration after losing a race here. Mike Smith told me last week, don't get so down, it's early. I told him, Mike, the first two races are over, wouldn't you be down if you were blanked the whole first week? He just looked at me and nodded. Jockeys understand the pain of losing. Not only do you lose

Jumpers soar over the first fence. *(Barbara D. Livingston)*

that individual race but future rides slip away with every loss. And that makes you kick the dog when you get home. I don't have a dog—he'd be too battered and bruised.

I usually end up looking for that dog here. I tend to strike out at Saratoga and would love to write a column about winning one. We'll see if tomorrow is the day. I got in trouble once for touting in the paper so let's just say my ride is a very nice horse, good personality, fine disposition, and has a chance tomorrow. I've actually never ridden him in a race. Don't really know what to expect. Sometimes that works to your advantage, because at least I don't have negative vibes. Like a first date, it might just turn out to be the one I marry. Yeah. That's the way to go into it anyway.

Today was the first dark day of the meet. They call them dark, but still I was up at five, like the rest of the backside, and up on Doc Martin before six. Rode Pebo's Guy after that. He's becoming my project for the month. He's a cool horse, nervous and not real confident about himself or anything around him. He trains in a set of earmuffs, like Gate Dancer's, except they're black. He's come a long way, I'll give him that. As a 2-year-old he would snowplow the shedrow when someone got on him, just take off sideways and collect anything in his wake. At least he doesn't do that anymore. Ride him real long (stirrups) and try to cajole him through what you want him to do. The longer your stirrups are, the more leg you have on the horse, the more you can guide the horse with pressure from your legs. Not a bad life philosophy. Ride long and try to get along.

If I'm thinking how wonderful it is to be in Saratoga again while I ride him, he will putter along like a pony. If I'm thinking about how much weight I have to lose in the next two days or how bad my head hurts from the night before, his sonar says tilt. Today we were somewhere in between. I have to lose a couple of pounds, I stayed in last night and I'm a deadline ahead.

My third horse was Brendan Shine. One of those Cadillac rides that makes what I do for a living seem like it's not what I do for a living. Like a rock. Great ride. Trainer Pat Byrne saw him this morning, and said, "Wow, he'd make a jumper, look at all that dashboard to put your feet on." The horse has dashboard, great seat, good engine.

Flaxen mane and tail—we'll be fighting over Brendan Shine around the barn.

I ran into Karl Keegan, who used to gallop for trainer Mike Hushion last summer. Hushion won the New York Derby at Finger Lakes with David over the weekend. Karl took credit: "I always told him he was a Derby horse." Kentucky, New York, a derby's a derby.

Speaking of New York: You can take the New York out of Saratoga but you can't take the Saratoga out of New York. You can claim a picnic table at eight in the morning, spread your blanket, your cooler, your picnic and come back in four hours and there it remains. You can look people in the eye at Saratoga, get to know strangers, leave your bike unlocked.

Then New York makes certain that you know you're still in New York. On opening day, I walked up to a couple of gentlemen, and I use the term lightly, who had circled a bunch of tables together, posted a "Private Party" sign on the tree, and had enough beer to start their own brewery. I wandered up, put on my best "Hey guys" face and asked them how they were doing. They said, "OK, what do you want?" Which, in turn, left me a little uneasy, but I went ahead and told them I was writing a book about Saratoga. They looked at me and the leader succinctly said, "We're not saying nothing. You got a wire? We're not saying nothing." Alrighty then, but you're missing the Saratoga theme and do you mind if I place this wire around your Brooklyn neck?

The theme, for those of you who don't know, is Another Day in Paradise. That's what trainer Tony Reinstedler declared on the way from his barn to the track this morning. He's right. This is paradise. With a price.

Another friend said to me, "I always look forward to Saratoga, then I get here and all it is is pain."

As usual, the truth lies somewhere in between. Everyone puts so much pressure on themselves that emotions get high and patience runs low. This is the one place every owner, trainer, jockey, horse, veterinarian, blacksmith, fan, bettor—every person on the grounds—wants to be a success. That exacts a toll.

I remember seeing Angel Cordero ride here for so many summers. He would be so aggressive, so intent on winning, it was like he was possessed—he would tell you that the place inspired him.

That's one way to look at every person up here, we are like Angel. Sometimes we move too soon because of it, sometimes we might shut off a friend, sometimes we might overdo it. That happens at Saratoga.

It isn't all good at Saratoga. It isn't all bad at Saratoga. But it's how you deal with both that makes your meet.

STOP AND TAKE IT IN
Wednesday, August 4

Come to the jocks' room, there's Jerry Bailey, Pat Day, Mike Smith, Jose Santos. All with "corners" set up for the meet. Photos. Name plaques. Spare tack. Spare clothes. They ride the card, pick up a five-digit check every Friday. Go home to their rented houses and wake up at Saratoga every morning. You could cut your finger on the creases in their clothes.

Now meet Pat Johnson.

The 40-year-old Kentucky-based jockey flew to town this morning for the Honorable Miss Handicap, a sprint for older fillies and mares. He arrived before the first race, for a 5:15 p.m. ride. One bag in tow, looking for a corner of his own. Johnson took a shower, sat around, watched races, handicapped his race, went over his plan, sat around, watched races, handicapped his race, went over his plan.

At 2:10, he was sitting in the jocks' room kitchen, by himself, leaning against the wall, *Racing Form* on the table. At 4:22, he was sitting in the jocks' room kitchen, by himself, leaning against the wall, *Racing Form* on the table.

So a conversation was started.

What's it like to ride here?

"It's OK. I can't actually put it into good words; as far as aura, it's old stuff anymore," Johnson said about his fifth or sixth trip to Saratoga. "The first time it was interesting, now I'm more concerned about winning the race and hopefully generating more business."

What have you been doing since you've been in the jocks' room?

"For me I think about what I could do, because there really isn't too much to do. I take a nap, but when you're awake it's tough to take naps. Watch the races and see if you can pick anything up."

You would be looking for some kind of bias or trend, how the racetrack is playing?

"Yeah, you try to pick up on how speed's holding and consider your horse and how she might run to how other horses have been running."

Who's the best horse you have ever ridden?

"I don't have one. I've won a bunch of Grade Twos and Threes but I don't really have a Grade One horse."

Why did you become a jockey?

"I chose to be a jockey over college. Growing up in the country, I liked animals and being fortunately small in stature I wanted to be a jockey, so that's what I did."

Was it the right decision?

Bourbon Belle and Pat Johnson. *(Barbara D. Livingston)*

"It's got to be now. I don't know what I would have done in college. Yeah, I'm satisfied—put it that way—with the decision to ride."

What would it be like to win a race here?

"Do you want an honest answer? It would be like $6,000. That's the truth."

So the magic of Saratoga doesn't affect you?

"It sounds, maybe condescending, but to me it's that way. I can go into other details but I would rather not."

Why?

"Because I should have been here 15 years ago. Business is business and it's the horses you ride that make the difference and I should have been here 15 years ago. I wasn't and I'm not now. I'm just here to ride the horse."

If you win this race, will your answers change about winning a race at Saratoga?

"No, without a doubt. You could almost get 'I told you so.' "

If you win this race I want you to stop and look into the infield, look across the lake at Saratoga, the revered Travers canoe and everything and go "I won a race at Saratoga." OK? Will you do that?

"Well sure. I'll do it."

Just take it in.

"Told you. That's right. Told you."

All right, good luck.

"What was your first name again?"

Sean.

Finally, five hours after he arrived, it was time for the riders to come out of the room and walk to the paddock. The first jockey? Pat Johnson.

No autographs (no one asked), just one stop to talk to old friend Richard DePass, Jorge Chavez's agent, and into the paddock for the feature.

Johnson boarded Bourbon Belle and the story became the story. Bourbon Belle broke quickly and got quicker. She won by herself.

This dreamer/journalist started yelling after the first quarter. All the way until my friend Bill grabbed my elbow and said "You're home free."

So was Johnson. My new friend Pat Johnson won his $6,000. He galloped Bourbon Belle back to the finish line and . . .

Stopped, turned her to the infield and just stood there. Taking it in.

After the photos, the weigh-in, and a couple of high-fives, Johnson came over and shook my hand, laughed and said "I have to say this . . . I told you so."

We laughed together in the winner's circle at Saratoga. I'm not exactly sure what Johnson meant with his I told you so, nor should you be sure. Each time I think about it, another motive comes into mind. You can see it any way you want. I do.

I still had one more question, so I stopped by the jocks' room again. Johnson was coming out of the shower, towel wrapped around him, soap dish in one hand, smile still wide across his face.

"Didn't you see, I did that just for you. Sean. Sean. Sean," Johnson said. "You helped. It was inspiring."

Yes it was. My question was answered.

GIVING

Thursday, August 5

Need more inspiration?

As I headed to the winner's circle to see Bourbon Belle and my man Pat, an entourage came down the steps from the boxes. Young girls, old men and one crying/cheering woman.

Meet Susan Bunning.

She's the daughter of trainer Peter Salmen Jr., the sister of breeder Peter Salmen III and the co-owner of Bourbon Belle. Part of a family that runs a five-horse operation—including broodmares and a full-brother in the September sale (she wanted me to put that in).

She was shaking, crying, smiling, swirling as she headed for her first trip to the Saratoga winner's circle.

"I thought she was going out too fast, I kinda stopped looking when I saw the fractions and then she does it so easy, it's scary. It's

Bourbon Belle posing for all the little people. *(Barbara D. Livingston)*

fun, she's so special to us. We're not real big-time, in the race with us are all the big-time folks, so it's just kind of overwhelming when she does it here.

"It's the first time we've ever been here and she won and it's great. I never thought I'd be here so it's as good as it gets, I guess. It really is. She's tough. She's a very special horse, we take care of her like you wouldn't believe. She shipped up here in a 15-horse van and she was the only one in it.

"We had to fly our jockey up this morning. All the people we believe in we brought here. It was great.

"We owned the stallion Whitesburg and bred the mother. It's just generations of families, we're all in it together. It's a family line that we've just stuck with.

"I almost physically fall apart because I'm so attached to this horse—mentally and emotionally. She's been so good to our family and every time she goes out there and puts such an effort for us. It's like a personal thing that she has just done. I just appreciate her so much I guess is the only way of putting it. I just don't ever take her for granted.

"It's like your heart is there, you're just like 'I can't believe you, you try every time.' She's the best. We'll never forget this time of our lives. I'll never ever ever forget it. I'm not silly enough to think that you get here that often on a thousand-dollar stud fee.

"Write in there, for anybody that still has that little bit of hope that maybe, that it does happen—I don't know how often it happens, but it happens on occasion. Tell all the little people not to give up."

I let her talk, nothing like a euphoric moment when people just let it out. So absolutely inspiring. Victory Gallop and Behrens. Pat Johnson and Susan Bunning. The (inspirational) leaders thus far.

I listened to what she said again on my tape recorder as I waited for the last race, when she was through talking and on her way to the Trustees' Room for champagne, the tape switched to what was recorded before her. For a split second I didn't know who was talking, then I realized it was D. Wayne Lukas talking about Cape Town winning the Florida Derby in 1998 (no, I don't use this tape recorder very often). Made me realize, even more, what Susan Bunning meant when she talked about the little people against the big people. Don't ever give up. It does happen. And don't ever take it for granted when it does.

As for my career, it's anything but inspiring. Yankee Stadium struck me out again. I finished fourth, ran pretty well, just had to use my horse up a little more than I wanted to keep position, and was out of horse at the head of the stretch. Tomorrow—I write this at 10:04 p.m. Wednesday—I ride Approaching Squall in the A.P. Smithwick, a $50,000 stakes. Here's hoping that Approaching Squall lands himself ahead of Victory Gallop, Behrens, Pat Johnson and Susan Bunning on our inspirational list.

WALK THIS WAY

Friday, August 6

Did I ever tell you about my walk? This was last Saturday night but worth retracing.

I had just seen Victory Gallop cool out at his barn, watched Elliott Walden blow dirt out of the Whitney winner's eyes. Always amazes me what these precious animals do for our entertainment. They have to have their eyes blown out after a race. Literally, you open their eyes wide with your fingers and blow out the dirt. Looks painful but better than spending the night with eyes full of sand.

I watched Victory Gallop all the way back to his barn where he finally looked at ease after his Whitney masterpiece. He caught drips of water off his nose when he had a bath, walked under the trees, and posed for photographer Barbara Livingston and her cronies.

It always awes me how the good ones know they are being watched. They pose for the attention. Bring out a camera or a crowd and they instantly become regal and enchanting.

I started to walk back to my car (had to be past seven by now), my job complete. Walden's barn is about halfway down the backside of the main track. So I wandered out of the trees and looked both ways. A long walk whichever direction I chose. It felt like my car was back in Pennsylvania. I thought about cutting across the infield but it probably wouldn't have made much difference. Of all the people I know in Saratoga, not one happened to drive by as I was searching for an easy way to get home. Now, I'm glad for the lack of taxi service. Still in coat, tie, loafers. Still carrying my mobile phone, tape recorder, *Form*, notepad, program, pens, money, digital camera, two sets of sunglasses and whatever paraphernalia you might find in a navy blazer. So I started walking.

Pick a side—I chose right and ran into Seth Gregory, Mark Hennig's assistant, heading back to the barn with Destruction. Walked the other way with him, talking about Succeed, showing off the photos of his first race (more paraphernalia). So I was right back where I started. I walked the other way this time.

I looked down at my shoes; they were polished for the start of this day, about eight hours ago. Now they looked camel brown, pure dust. Made me wonder about a day at Saratoga. I started out primped and pristine, and finished walking by myself around the racetrack. I felt like walking straight to the cleaners and dumping off what was on my body. After that—a shower, a porch and a cold beer.

You're not alone—even when the seats are empty—at Saratoga.
(Harlan Marks)

But still I walked. I passed a couple of grooms heavy into Budweiser. They looked at me, waved, and wondered if I was lost or just couldn't find my car. I felt lost, in a good way. I could have stopped for a Bud, but kept walking. The sprinklers were in full force in the center of the racetrack, the water trucks and harrows erased today's exploits and prepared for tomorrow's. I walked.

It is a long walk. Past the gate, which now rests for the night, past a Pinkerton security guard waiting to direct traffic, past the small training track at Clare Court, past the Horse Shoe Inn on Nelson Avenue.

Music blared from the Horse Shoe. Made me stop and wonder who was in there and who was out here. I was alone and thinking about this glorious town. Thinking about how I might find the words for Victory Gallop and Behrens. I agonize at the thought of how to do it justice, if the words will show up. So I walked, listened to a few bars of "How Sweet It Is to Be Loved by You," even sang a few lines. Bad song when you're alone.

So I walked along Nelson Avenue, still under the cover of trees, and tried to make eye contact with a few fans heading home for the day. Some looked pained, others content. I bounced between both.

Eventually I passed three kids hanging on the outside rail just past the wire. Thought they might enlighten me.

Remember when Chris McCarron said, "Saratoga is class, excitement, and history"?

Roberto Mack, age 11, from Brooklyn, had this to say: "It's quieter, easier and less violent."

That's why he likes Saratoga. Simple really. The chasm of life between McCarron's California existence and Roberto's New York being.

Justin chimed in with, "They give away hats here."

Roberto was with his cousins Reinaldo, 9, and Justin Mack, 11. Their fathers are peace officers, they said with pride. They had to say "peace officers" a hundred times.

The three kids asked me as many questions as I could ask them.

"Why are you writing this down?"

"Is this going to be in all the papers?"

"You got a wife?"

"What kind of car do you drive?"

"What time do you write your stuff?"

We just talked. Horses and kids, the epitome of innocence.

"We have to learn more so we can get good jobs," Roberto said. "I want to be an architect because I know how to draw. I'm not that good, but I always try."

They talked about Brooklyn and how loud it is there, they took a picture with me, they hung on the rail and talked. Adults walked past and shook their heads, wondered what the man in the tie and blazer was doing talking to these three kids. I couldn't help but wonder if their bewilderment would have been different if these kids were white.

My new friends kept talking.

"In Saratoga, like, you can put your bike in the sidewalk and they won't steal it," Reinaldo said. "We like the horses here. They're friendly. We get to ride them sometimes."

For their sake, I hope they do. If we were only as smart as these three.

"I never want to smoke or bet when I grow up," Reinaldo said. "You die easier if you do that."

"If I drink beer, I would only drink once a week or maybe never," Roberto said.

"Don't fall into other people's footsteps," Roberto told me.

Think about that one.

I walked away a whole lot lighter than I walked up to Justin, Reinaldo and Roberto.

As I traveled through the racetrack, past the sweepers and rakers who were cleaning up old tickets and popcorn boxes, I couldn't help but feel revived. Kids (and horses) do that to you. As I walked through the post-party, a band of "adults" came sauntering past me, about six men, coolers and chairs under arms and the beer still flowing.

I looked at them and asked, "How was your day, win or lose?"

The one in the front took a swig from his green label and bellowed, "Doesn't matter. Doing better than you—nice coat."

Guess they lost—more than they could ever count.

Thursday was a drag as I finished third on Approaching Squall. Ran well, wish I had Wednesday's trip on Thursday's horse. That's always the way. I feel the meet slipping away (as a jockey), four races down, no winners and not that much to look forward to. Tough place to win, but at least I'm losing at Saratoga.

FRAGILITY

Saturday, August 7

This is the one I didn't want to write.

But somehow I knew I would have to. I was just hoping it would be later than sooner. Succeed is retired.

The greatest racehorse that ever lived is no longer a racehorse. It's my job to find him a good home now. That's the positive. Succeed is going to be a foxhunter or a show horse or someone's pet. Maybe all three. The grind is over for him; he gets out.

It breaks my heart. I could look at it a hundred different ways.

None work. They all have their credence, but all leave me empty, too.

I could say it was a big waste of time. The greatest experience in the world. The most frustrating. The most disappointing. The most fulfilling. The most deflating. The most emotional. The most work. The most fun. The most educational.

I spent 10 months with Succeed. I taught him how to jump and how to trust. He taught me patience, confidence, decision-making, understanding. He taught me, or showed me, how absolutely brilliant a horse can be. For that, I will forever carry him in my heart.

Horses run and jump. Horses also become projects. Friends. Reasons to get out of bed.

I met Succeed at Gulfstream Park two winters ago and he became my inspiration. Sounds so hokey, but the horse has all the presence, all the class, all the mystique you would ever want in a species. Pick the one person in the world that you would like to meet. I just had that for 10 months.

I ran him in his first jumping race on July 25, he finished second, was head and head at the last and just got a little tired. You read all about it.

Succeed came out of his race seemingly fine. We gave him Bute, poultice and rest. He was proud of himself. But there was a little filling in his right suspensory. It just wouldn't go away. As much as I tried to ignore it or improve it, the leg just didn't seem right. When you look at a horse's leg 10 times a day for 10 months, you know every hair, every bump, every vein. It becomes your leg. And you know in your gut when something's wrong. I rode him a couple of times, he was sound and full of himself. I'll never forget my rides on Succeed at Saratoga. I finally gave in and ultrasounded the leg on Thursday. Sean, meet your maker. I'll give you the exact words:

History: Right front chronic thickening in proximal palmar metacarpal region. No lameness associated with swelling.

Physical Exam Findings: Thickening of right front metacarpal region; most pronounced along medial aspect of leg. No heat/sensitivity on palpation.

Sonographic Findings: Decrease in degree of echogenicity/fiber alignment of medial aspect of right front distal suspensory ligament body; fiber disruption continues distally throughout length of medial suspensory branch. Normal appearance of right front lateral suspensory branch. Normal appearance of right front SDF/DDF tendons, ICL.

Diagnosis: Desmitis of right front suspensory ligament body. Desmitis of right front medial suspensory branch with core lesion.

Recommendations: Stall rest with handwalking for next eight to 12 weeks. No turn-out. Daily cold hosing, ice therapy. Bute/Naquasone for next one to two days.

Succeed plowed plenty of snow on his way.
(Elizabeth Hendriks)

That's the clinical side. I already told you the personal side. I want to tear up the piece of paper with all that disappointment written on it. You knew what I thought of the horse; it's just so empty calling it a day. When you've been riding races for as long as I have (12 years), horses like Succeed are why I still do it. I wanted to win one race on him. He almost did it. We came so close. The good thing is I at least found out that he was as good as I thought. I got to feel it. So it was worth it just for that.

I've never been married, never had kids—Succeed sufficed for both for a short time. My biggest fear in training Succeed was the possibility of having to look him in the eye and tell him his life was over. Now I have to look him in the eye and tell him his life as a race-horse is over. And you know what, he's taking it much better than I. All he ever wanted to be was someone's pet.

People say horses deserve the chance to show us how good they are. Succeed just wants to eat grass and go for fun rides. That's what he gets to do now. And he is the best at both.

If you ever ask, Succeed is the greatest I have ever ridden. Better than Victorian Hill, the leading steeplechase money earner for years. Better than To Ridley, with whom I won the Carolina Cup, the Iroquois and the Temple Gwathmey stakes. Better than Red Raven (but it's damn close), my race pony who was the first to ever make me feel important. Better than Fourstardave, Hodges Bay or any other horse I ever had the privilege of knowing.

To me, he's the best.

I accomplished nothing on him—and everything.

Succeed

If *Saratoga Days* was a whim, then Succeed was a dream.

And I owe it all to one sentence: "I've got a horse I want you to ride while I'm gone . . . I think you'll like him"—Mark Hennig's assistant Ellie, February 1998, Gulfstream Park.

I rode him, I loved him, and I began to think big.

At least Saratoga big. Of course, thinking big has always been Succeed's curse.

When Harbor View Farm breeds you and Flawlessly, a $2.5 million earner and two-time Eclipse Award winner, is your full-sister, people think big from the day you hit the ground. Especially when you look and move like Succeed.

"We were thinking Triple Crown after he won as a 2-year-old. We were excited," said owner Patrice Wolfson in Saratoga in 1998.

Ankle injuries, tendon strains, foot problems and a scattered 0-for-4 followed that dream.

Succeed glided into my heart as soon as I sat on him. Before I had made the eighth of a mile walk from Mark Hennig's barn to the Gulfstream Park track, I knew this horse was one of a kind.

He's one of those that allows you to ride him. Like it's a privilege, a present, out of his sheer generosity. Talk about going for a joyride.

Of course he intimidated me, awed me and pretty much scared me every time Mark gave me a leg up on the highlight of my day from February to March 1998. Heck, every time I looked at the horse. He was the first horse I took any notice of when I walked down Mark's shedrow on my first day. He stuck his long head out at

Succeed never looked better than the day he made it to the Saratoga paddock. *(Elizabeth Hendriks)*

me, from behind a full screen. I'll never forget jumping across the barn and looking at him: "Who the hell are you?" From that moment on I was a starstruck kid any time I was near Succeed.

I remember leaving Florida. I was there for only six weeks writing for *The Blood-Horse,* and thinking the thing I'll miss the most is that horse—Succeed. I know, I know, I spent two months with the sun, the beach and horses like Skip Away and Lil's Lad and some non-winners-of-a-race-other-than four-year-old is what I'll remember.

Succeed is a big bay with a white star on the greatest head I've ever seen. And his eyes look right into your heart, like your first love. Walk up the shedrow, pop out of the tackroom, come back from the kitchen during the break, Succeed would see me. He was the barn surveillance system.

He's one of those creatures I just like to look at. I've never seen the Grand Canyon but I assume I'd stand on its precipice and get the same feeling I get when I look into Succeed's eyes.

I like all horses. Succeed, for whatever reason, is the greatest horse I've ever known. That's why I begged, pleaded and finally convinced Mark and the Wolfsons to send Succeed to me.

When you truly believe something, you can convince anybody of anything. But you have to be absolute in your belief.

I had two goals when he came to me, win one race and find him a good home.

I believed the horse would be a good jumper. He's smart. He's athletic. He's light on his feet. He's got a sense of humor. He wants to be entertained. He has amazing eyesight. He never gets tired. He's nimble. As graceful as Peggy Fleming and as powerful as Dick Butkus.

The biggest question was would he stay sound? It was a catch-22: if he was sound he wouldn't be here, so I took him any way I could, and that's about the way he is.

Before Gulfstream, Succeed bowed his left front tendon and broke a bone in his foot. In between Hennig and Clancy was ankle surgery. A chip was removed from his left front ankle and a couple of old ones were discovered, ground up in the ankle.

Succeed and I scout out the first fence. *(Elizabeth Hendriks)*

Dr. Stephen Selway, who did the surgery, termed it "reasonably optimistic" to race again. That was good enough for me.

So physically he was a question. Mentally, he was always a little soft. He just doesn't know how good he is, how easily he does things and how quickly he could rule the world. You know, the genius who is so smart he questions everything and can't capitalize on his brilliance.

We worked on Succeed's toughness. I turned him out this winter for two hours in the rain with Due North, who was so tough he ran over 100 times and won nearly a million dollars before becoming the grouchiest lead pony that ever lived.

We did our best flat work and tried to make Succeed soft and supple. All that good stuff. He was naturally quite good at it already, I can't take the credit there. Having a horse carry himself in a balanced frame is one of the most important aspects of racing and probably the most overlooked. I tried to not overlook it with Succeed. I wanted him to carry his head down and use his hind end, so we could take some of the pressure off his front legs. With all of Succeed's problems, any little thing would help. This was delicate work.

I promised to not overlook anything with Succeed. As Bill Mott says, "When they give you the information, I think you're expected to use it." I have all the information. Succeed gave it to me.

He also gave me some incredible days along the way.

October 7, the day Succeed became my horse, I met Andy Simoff's van at 8 p.m. I hadn't seen Succeed since Belmont Stakes week when I had my last ride on him. I was supposed to be covering Real Quiet and Victory Gallop, but the absolute highlight of the week was riding my old friend around the masterpiece oval at Belmont Park. So here I was greeting him at Ricky and Lizzie Hendriks' barn in Cochranville, Pa., five months later. Would I recognize him? Would he recognize me?

The van finally arrived. Every horse van in the world shows up an hour after they tell you to expect them. Tommy Pointer opened the van door.

There he was, all wrapped up in white cloth. Around his halter, so he wouldn't rub his precious face, and around all four legs, for the same reason. Succeed, my old boy, welcome to my world. I snapped a rope shank on his halter; Pointer told me to be careful, "He's a goofy bugger." Inside my head, I scoffed, this is my horse, he'll follow me anywhere, and Succeed followed me down the ramp like he knew this was his chance. Maybe horses don't ever think like this, but if you think like that, they follow your lead. Maybe they can't rationalize it all, but they understand who is in their corner.

Succeed skipped off the van into the darkness and did what I love about him, he started grazing. Head down in the green grass. I knew I loved this horse. It was like seeing an old friend who went off to war, or just got a divorce. I settled him into the five-stall barn, last stall on the left. He stretched out for a leak and then rolled in his straw bed. Took a drink, stuck his head out the window and then dove into the pile of alfalfa hay. People can't understand horses? What do you do after a long trip, especially if you had to stand the whole time? Succeed and I, would grab a snack as we walk through the kitchen, go to the bathroom, roll around in our new bed, swig down a cold drink, look out the window at our new digs, then dive

into a big meal. Me, you, Succeed, no difference.

I fed him carrots and took his bandages off (like taking off your shoes and socks). Then I sat in the corner and marveled at the boy who came home.

Now this is the life: Succeed doing what he does best. *(Elizabeth Hendriks)*

He looked smaller than I remembered. Not as grand looking, mostly because he was in training when I last saw him, but just as familiar. He stuck his nose down into my lap as I leaned against his new wall. I was supposed to meet everybody at the Country Place Deli for a beer and to watch the steeplechase races from the week before. I felt at home right there—I've never had children but when I do, I expect it will be a lot like this. I just sat and watched him jaw hay. He picked his head up and looked at me every once in a while, but he was pretty content, could've been the hay, but I like to think it was me.

Eventually Ricky, Lizzie, Fenneka, and Geoff Turnbull came home from the movies and were introduced to Succeed. I instantly made excuses for him even though they for the most part thought he was cool. He stuck his nose in all their faces and wondered if we would do this every night.

I don't know why I felt self-conscious as they looked at him. It was like they were looking at me. I had been talking about the horse since February and knew how much I thought of him, so I guess I just wanted them to think the same way.

Succeed settled in, even if 3-year-old Liza Hendriks called him the Cwazy Horse. He had a pressing desire to see how much of his body he could fit through the two-foot square window in the back of his stall. He would stick his head through like he was coming out. Some days I had to just walk away in fear. I could just see the cwazy horse running around the yard with the barn hanging around his neck.

Stall rest is brutal for horses. They just get bored, and a thousand pounds of boredom can be quite a sight. Succeed provided plenty of those during his rest stop.

The day he stuck his leg over the Port A' Pad was a keeper. A Port A' Pad is a wire mesh paddock designed for safe turnout of horses. It's as high as your bedroom wall and the safest barrier you can put around a Thoroughbred horse other than a stall.

So Succeed would go out in his Port A' Pad every day while he recuperated from the ankle surgery. One pretty fall afternoon, he was in his safe sanctuary when he decided to do his Silver (as in Hi-Ho . . .) impersonation, went straight up and pawed the air like an ancient Greek warrior horse, only to hang his leg on the top of the Port A' Pad. There was my all-time greatest horse hopping around on his hind legs with one front leg stuck on the top of an eight-foot fence. You should have seen his face.

What do you do? Here's your 1,000-pound dream suspended on a wire fence. All I could think was what a stupid way for it to all end.

Succeed hopped and danced for about five seconds while I stood mouth agape waiting for the horse or the fence or both to break. But not my trusty Succeed—he managed one final hoist and popped himself off with a dismount that would have made Bart Connor proud. So that was the first of many cringing moments from Succeed.

The exhilarating ones outnumbered the cringing.

You can drive someone's Rolls Royce. Then you can drive your own. Riding horses when someone else is in charge of them is easy. You don't make the final decision, you provide information and opinions but it's always advising, not deciding.

I brought Succeed to Fair Hill Training Center in December 1998 and went for a ride. Around the shedrow of Parlo Six. We walked and tried not to be nervous. We were starting at ground zero and I was in charge now. Think of your greatest hope, dream, pride and then throw some tack over it and jump on for its first exercise in six months.

Succeed liked the attention. Horses like activity. They miss a routine when they go from training every day to stall rest. Succeed walked around the barn like a foxhound when he gets out of the hound truck at the meet. Part curiosity, part exuberance. I jogged him around the shed a few times. He liked that. You can ride horses and then you can ride horses. When I ride a horse like this, I can feel my insides tense up. I keep telling myself, "Relax or he'll sense your anxiety." My legs and hands are doing what they are supposed to be doing but my body, my gut, is on a different plain.

Lizzie stepped gingerly up to the edge of the shedrow as I passed and asked how things were going. My lips parted just enough for a slight smirk, no sound came out. That's the feel Succeed gave me, verbally paralyzed, like any sound might destroy the moment. He's a horse you talk about when you're safely and firmly on the ground.

I rode him in what was deemed the slunch. It's basically riding the same way as usual, soft hands, strong leg, but you "slunch" trying to one yourself with the horse. This is not a performance technique—it's for survival. You try to lose all the space between your head and your feet. Eventually my confidence rose while I rode Succeed and I was able to actually sit up like a real rider. It helped that I had slunched for the first two weeks in Florida and was on the same schedule this time.

We set up some rails in the shedrow to see how the greatest horse in the world jumped. He never jumped in his life, other than when he leapt off the ground for kicks back at Gulfstream. But somehow I knew he would jump for fun.

Part logic, part intuition. Both right.

Jumping Succeed was simpler than tying your shoes. He just jogged, cantered, walked toward the obstacle and hopped over it. He was never scared, never hesitant, never less than pure fluency.

His first jump came on December 5, 1998. We stepped over a log in the woods. It was all of about one foot high and he cleared it. I've never sat on a better jumper, he just jumped everything so effortlessly, not that it was a surprise.

Succeed just makes you feel like you can ride. And in this day and age, that's probably the most important thing a horse can do for a human.

When Succeed jumps he provides an instant in mid-air to feel it. His body comes up to the rider's chest and he arcs in a perfect rhythmical motion.

Some horses can't get their legs together to jump. Some horses instantly get on the defensive when introduced to jumping. Most eventually get the hang of it. Succeed understood the principle and was looking for the next question before we could even think of it.

Maybe Bruce Miller would say the same thing about all-time leading steeplechase earner Lonesome Glory. Maybe Carl Hanford would say Kelso was a step ahead of everyone around him. I'm sure Cigar, Shergar and Phar Lap could have jumped better than Dwight Stones. But no one ever asked them.

I asked Succeed and he answered every time. Stones is a chump next to Succeed.

We jumped logs in the woods, small chicken coops, show fences in an indoor arena. It was like he had been there before. God must have taught him to jump before he sent him this way.

I'll never forget the rides I had on Succeed in the winter of '98–99. Around Fair Hill, the white-tailed deer outnumber horses and people. Succeed saw his first deer, and stopped and glared at the new creature. Most horses head the other direction—Succeed's heart pounded down by my foot but he never moved away, he actually went toward the discovery.

Succeed could make Monty Roberts out of Vince McMahon.

We took Succeed and a couple of other young jumpers to an indoor arena near Unionville that winter. He walked into the place like he built it. Gave leads to all the other horses who were completely taken aback at the imposing building. We jumped over fake stone walls, poles and blocks.

Riding Succeed is simply easier than riding other horses.

He makes you good.

I took my brother, Joe, along for Succeed's first stream crossing. I wanted to make sure Succeed had a chance to take a look at a stream before he was in a big set of horses who would leave him behind.

It was Monty Roberts.

We came to a small stream in the woods. Joe and Due North ambled through the water. Succeed hesitated and snorted at the crossing.

If you have ever ridden a horse, you will understand me when I say I knew he would cross it but it might take a minute. He researched it. Took a look at the situation. He inched closer, all the time with his head down looking at his newest assignment. He even "licked and chewed" like Roberts talks about in his book. Joe and I both just sat and watched. Eventually without a kick or yell or slap, Succeed made his decision and walked through the stream. I'll never forget the sheer intelligence of the horse at that moment. He was so proud of himself after walking through the water obstacle. Joe was on the bandwagon now also.

See why Succeed had everyone he touched thinking big?

Thinking big and jumping big. When I rode Succeed, I pointed him at anything. I followed another son of Affirmed, named Ratify, over a huge log in a hedgerow, bigger than what you would normally jump a green horse over; he flew it.

He just cantered down in perfect rhythm and soared over a three-foot log. It was the landing that was remarkable. His feet touched the ground like a ballerina's and out of pure pride he just took off to the top of the hill. His body underneath me was just bellowing out how good he felt. I never felt a horse touch the ground like Succeed, like feather on fog.

When we pulled up next to Ratify, I couldn't speak. Awe is a silencer.

Then I messed up the big horse. It was a rainy day at Fair Hill and Succeed and Ratify got into a fight. Ratify won. He kicked the big horse in the hind leg while they were turned out together. I had overlooked something, it was my fault and I'll never forgive myself.

We eventually had to do surgery to clean out the wound. I walked into New Bolton Center to see my friend wrapped from foot to stifle in Ace bandage. You know when that involuntary cry mechanism goes off in you. He looked so pathetic.

Remember when I wrote that Succeed could look right through you? I was nothing but smoke when I saw him there. I'd make a bad dad. When I hurt myself as a child, my dad would look at me with that concerned-but-not-to-worry face. Dad's demeanor said everything would be OK. Succeed got none of that from me.

The wild thing was that Dad was with me, telling me he would be fine. And you know what? Dad made it better again.

Succeed was about two or three weeks away from his first flat race when he got kicked—well maybe a month, but he was training as well as any horse could ever train. The leg healed but we missed the spring season and that's why he was making his first start of the year at Saratoga.

It would have been a lot easier in the spring when the ground was soft and I could have given him a prep race at one of the jump meets.

But we made it to Saratoga. That's where Succeed deserved to run his last race. Now all we can do is laugh about the deer we watched in December. The snow we kicked in January. The logs we jumped in February. The idle stall hours in March and April. The poultice we used in May. The woodchips we galloped over in June. The bullet works in July. The race at the end of July. The easy days for the rest of his life.

And the chapter in *Saratoga Days*.

WALKING HOTS
Sunday, August 8

"Boy, you're late. What happened, you get stuck in the Parting Glass?"

Well . . .

That's how Carl Nafzger greeted me this morning. I set up a hotwalking session with Banshee Breeze, winner of Saturday's Go For Wand Stakes, for 6:30. Plans are so easy to make the day before and so hard to keep the day of.

I arrived at 6:38, and since it's Sunday—I will confess—I did get stuck in the Parting Glass. I managed to break out at 2 a.m., walked past the motion light on Lake Avenue that scares me every night, while my in-town-for-a-day friends Wass and Jeff went on to the next trap. That's what kills you at Saratoga, the people who are sleeping 'til noon. (I just came home, off three hours sleep, and Wass is still sprawled out on the floor. He'll get up at noon and wonder why I'm grumpy and need a nap while he wants to go for lunch and the first).

I tried to make three hours of sleep seem like eight. It didn't work, and I was late for my hotwalking job. Banshee Breeze didn't seem to mind. She was done up past her knees and standing in the back of her stall munching away at a flake of alfalfa hay. Nafzger handed me Yukon, the lead pony. He won two of three (chances are his name wasn't Yukon then), got hurt and they made him the pony. Succeed, are you listening?

So I walked Yukon around the barn by a piece of bailing twine. He ate out of every hay net and feed tub in the shedrow. We stopped at

Banshee Breeze turns heads in the paddock. *(Elizabeth Hendriks)*

Banshee Breeze's stall and let Yukon eat out of her hay net. She didn't think much of that, although she was stealing from her neighbor's net herself. Horses are the ones who patented the phrase "The grass is always greener on the other side."

Nafzger said she came back well, explained that they had her only 95 percent for the race. She got a little tired, he said, but gutted it out. It was fun to meet her, she's a real-sweet looking filly, dainty, with a very feminine face. I found it intriguing that she was done for the day and it wasn't even 7 a.m.

Yukon ate some of her doughnuts and she ate an apple. Eventually she just turned around and tried to sleep, intent on ignoring the intruders.

I gathered that my hotwalking career was a demotion and had enough ribbing from an old girlfriend who works for Nafzger. So I headed back to the O'Brien stable after at least getting to meet Banshee Breeze.

I grabbed a cup of tea from the track kitchen and made my way back to Barn 61. Mr. O'Brien greeted me in much the same way

Nafzger did: "Long time no see."

I was a little late and soon I was drenched. Finally the rain came to Saratoga—another reason why I couldn't get out of bed.

Saratoga in the rain is something to behold. It pours here and no one ever seems ready for it. Most barns don't have covered shedrows, none of them seem to have gutters or rain spouts. The place was built with a "Some days it rains and some days you get wet" idea in mind. Backstretch people just strap on the gear and go through the same motions. The you-won't-melt theory.

Already a hardy group, racetrackers rise to their best when it rains It's like a duty, and they just slog through it. Around Leo's barn, he stays under the shed and gets a laugh when you come back soaked. Especially when you're late; it's basically an invitation for Leo to get you as wet as he can. I rode the pony on two sets and came home with a sore throat. Ah, it's a great life.

Now, do you want the "Only in Saratoga" story of the week?

"Mr. Rooney, tell me something inspirational about Saratoga," I asked the rumpled looking man who could have passed for Joe TwoDollar Bettor.

"Well, that's not a question. Geez, what a way to go at it. You're never going to make it. You've got to a have a question, a sensible question. That's not a question. What do you do for a living, you in school?"

I'm a steeplechase jockey and freelance writer, write my own newspaper.

"Yeah?"

Have you been coming here forever? I asked.

"Since I was in the fourth form at the Albany Academy. Once a year, that's all, just come once a year. I like it. I know Saratoga real well."

What do you like about it?

"Well, I'm not one for tradition but you have to be taken with looking around and thinking about how long this has been going on. I walk through the grandstand or down that lower area and I think 'My God, I did this 50 years ago.' "

Nothing's changed?

Banshee Breeze, flanked by her sisters Charm (left) and Unbridled Wind.
(Barbara D. Livingston)

"Yeah, it's good. You can't get hung up on how good things used to be, but still a lot of them were pretty good."

You bet?

"Oh sure, you have to bet."

Did you win today?

"No, you don't win most of the time."

That's why it still exists, right?

"Yeah."

Thanks, Mr. Rooney. Good night.

Yup, I ran into Andy Rooney of *60 Minutes* fame on the way out of the races and he told me I was never going to make it (guess he doesn't read www.thebackstretch.com). Every steeplechase trainer in the game has told me that at one time or another so what the heck, at least it was Andy Rooney. And what does he know anyway?

Maybe I'll send him a copy of the book.

HALL OF FAME
Monday, August 9

Listen to Mark Hennig present D. Wayne Lukas with his induction into The National Museum of Racing's Hall of Fame. Hennig along with present and former Lukas assistants Randy Bradshaw, son Jeff Lukas, Kiaran McLaughlin, Todd Pletcher and Dallas Stewart gave Lukas away at the Hall of Fame.

"Good morning. When we were first asked to present Wayne with this honor, we all began to explore the many memories and experiences we have had during our years of working with the world's most successful horse trainer.

"As you have just heard a number of statistical accomplishments of D. Wayne Lukas, we wanted to add some of the intangibles that cannot be recorded in the record books. So much has changed in our industry because of Wayne. The pride and beautification of our barns—many now have multiple divisions—the reality that any race is truly just one flight away. And let's not forget those white bridles, love them or hate them, they're here to stay.

"A lot of you are aware that Wayne was a coach and teacher many years ago. The six of us standing before you can attest that he never left these ranks. He simply chose to ply those trades within the horse industry. For those of us fortunate to know or work with Wayne, there is no doubt that he could have risen to the top of any chosen profession. The six of us have worked a combined 58 years for Wayne and as we began to reflect on the countless lessons that he has taught us through his leadership, the one thing that stuck out most in all of our minds was the team concept. 'THERE IS NO I IN TEAM,' Wayne would preach to us.

"He created an atmosphere amongst us that allowed for us to learn and grow as horsemen in our own right. He encouraged us to teach and appreciate each other, further strengthening the team concept. We still continue to this day to bounce ideas off one another. Wayne gave us the freedom to make our mistakes but was always there to praise and correct us.

Wayne Lukas (second from left) accepts congratulations from protégés Mark Hennig, Todd Pletcher, Kiaran McLaughlin, Randy Bradshaw, Dallas Stewart, and Jeff Lukas. *(Skip Dickstein)*

"His attention to detail is intense. Nothing can escape his scrutiny. One example that best illustrates the teacher in Wayne happened to myself, not long after I was given my first opportunity with a division. It was one of those cold, wet winter days at beautiful Aqueduct, and I had just saddled two winners. After checking the condition of the runners, I settled into the warmth of my D. Wayne Lukas Jeep, picked up my D. Wayne Lukas mobile phone and called the boss.

"'Hey Boss, they ran good.'

"Without a pause, on the other end of the phone, Wayne launched into an expletive-filled tirade—'Those horses didn't run good,' he said.

"'They both won, they ran good,' I stated again.

"'They didn't run good at all,' Wayne said.

"While I sat bewildered, an irate Wayne continued.

"'You have quality horses to train, and they are owned by people who have invested millions of dollars. If you want to communicate with owners, you and that hillbilly brother-in-law of yours need to learn something: HORSES DON'T RUN GOOD, THEY RUN WELL!'

"He then said congratulations on a job well done and we had a normal conversation about the day's activities. These types of lessons got passed along quickly and we would all learn from one another's mistakes. There is an endless list of lessons that we were taught in a matter of minutes.

"From his accomplishments on the track to the flowered barns and herringbone raked shedrows, D. Wayne Lukas has left a huge mark on the racing game. He has no peers when it comes to his accomplishments and he has changed this wonderful game of ours forever.

"Wayne, we are honored to stand here and represent not only your legacy but an entire industry that is forever grateful for what you bring to the court. Thanks to you, all of us standing here are doing real well and we are pleased to be the ones to tell you: You done good, Wayne."

Then the house came down, the packed Humphrey S. Finney sales pavilion clapped thunderously and laughed with all their might at Mark's punchline. It was the second time around for me.

I stopped by Mark's barn last week to talk about Succeed. He popped open his briefcase and handed me this speech. I guess he wanted my approval, which, when I laughed my head off, he got. At the end of the ceremony today, I skeefed the speech, figuring you ought to hear it word for word.

Lukas, love him or hate him (just like the bridles), predictably gave a great acceptance speech. This is what stood out:

"It's not always been blue skies and clear sailing in my career. It is my nature to push the envelope every time. If you want a coach that wants to walk the ball up the court you better get another guy because we're going to run and press every time.

"I have tried to pattern my life after an old country western song—sing like you don't need the money, dance as though nobody is watching and love like you'll never be hurt.

"When Winning Colors hit the front and I won the race, my first Kentucky Derby, I turned and said, 'My turn.' August 9, 1999, is my turn.

"What does it all mean? Whenever champions gather, and all

champions of different sports gather at any function, I'm just going to stand up and say I belong. Thanks."

That's the gist. Lukas is a master. The man knows how to succeed. You knew, walking into the pavilion today, that he would be flawless in his acceptance. He didn't disappoint. D. Wayne is the smoothest speaker since JFK.

Overshadowed by D. Wayne, but not underappreciated, jockey Russell Baze and horses Exceller, Miesque and Gun Bow were inducted also.

Baze gave a humbler speech, thanking his parents, whom he had to coax to stand up for their recognition, his wife and family, his agent, horsemen, and "my heavenly father."

Baze gave this account of his career: "I always thought I was just lucky to go to work every day for 25 years to a job I love."

The Hall of Fame induction never ceases to amaze. It's what is good in the sport. We sit a couple of seats behind half the Hall of Fame. You can get your photo with Baze, get your poster-sized Secretariat picture signed, talk to Lukas, steal the speech off Hennig. Our game is exactly that; our game. You just walk up to your heroes, whether it's walking to the paddock with Jerry Bailey or being within 10 feet of Angel Cordero kissing Ron Turcotte on the cheek at the induction.

Sometimes racing does do something for the fan. The Hall of Fame induction is one of those times.

NEW HOME
Tuesday, August 10

Catch-up day. Thank the racing gods for dark days. One day a week to pick your head up and see where you are. Me? I'm in my office, just out of bed, but don't tell anyone (especially at Leo O'Brien's barn). I slept in today. Half sick (riding in the rain will do that to you) and all the way tired. Decided to skip the first four sets and catch Proud Run (the horse) after the harrowing (of the track) break. The morning work, the writing, the races, the betting, the dieting, the running, the riding races, the entertaining, the socializing, the expectations—the Saratoga Decathlon. I'm still on my feet so I guess I'm winning. Or at least holding my own. I could not get out of bed today; it was simply impossible. My alarm went off for hours and I couldn't move.

I thought I would tell you about Russell Baze today. Two ss's and two ll's. I caught the now Hall of Fame jockey in the box seats after the eighth race yesterday. He had just presented the Hall of Fame Stakes trophy to Jerry Bailey, who rode Marquette to victory in the turf stakes.

Baze came to Saratoga with his wife, Tami, daughters Trinity, Brandi, and Cassie and son, Gable. Parents Joe and Susan traveled from Montana for the event. Joe was a former jockey, raising Russell on the circuit. He rode his first race a day before his 16th birthday on an Appaloosa at a fair in Walla Walla, Washington.

Baze relaxed in the corner of the five-seat box with his size 5½ shoes propped up on a chair. Adorned in his brand-new navy Hall of Fame blazer (37 short), Baze sat content and at ease. That's because the speech was over.

Russell Baze smiles from his new home. *(Skip Dickstein)*

"I had just a little time to think about [being inducted] before the introduction ceremony itself," Baze said. "I was sitting there thinking about giving the speech, but it was relatively painless."

Baze gave a real speech. When D. Wayne Lukas goes up to the podium, it's hard to associate with him; you just can't see yourself in him. No offense, either. Lukas is just so polished, the guy doesn't miss; he's a horse trainer in a politician's body. But when Russell Baze steps up, I don't know, it's more real. He thanked his family and the horsemen. Just like you would. Lukas is a showman, the best in the business; Baze is a working guy banging out a living.

Baze called the day hectic, like his lifestyle. He arrived in Saratoga at eleven Sunday night. A short trip for Baze, who will be back at work on Wednesday trying to reach 400 again. In 1998, Baze rode more than 400 winners for the seventh straight time, a record. Jockeys get to smile in the winner's circle and ride some of the greatest athletes in the world, but they don't dwell on it; Baze is at Saratoga on Monday and on the card in Northern California on Wednesday. Being a flat jockey was my dream—it's simply Russell Baze's life.

Baze remembered the day he got the call about being elected to the Hall of Fame. He couldn't tell anyone for a week; of course he told his wife, Tami, before the phone left his ear. That has to be the best part of marriage, sharing momentous occasions, or I guess just sharing yourself with one other person.

Baze felt honored just to be nominated.

"The phone call was great but when I first heard that I was nominated it was really a surprise; I never thought anybody would think of me in that context," Baze said. "I was surprised they elected me this year because there were some worthy riders nominated."

Baze was introduced at his induction as the hero of the two-dollar bettor.

"I look at myself as more of a blue-collar type guy than a white-collar guy who gets to ride the big horses in the big races, which is fine with me. I just love the game, I love riding, I enjoy winning on a cheap horse just as much as a stakes horse," Baze said. "The converse is not the same. It hurts more to get beat on a good horse than a cheap horse."

Baze called Event of the Year the best horse he's ever ridden. Ask him if this is the culmination.

"Gee, I hope not. This is as high as a guy can go, but I hope it's not downhill from here," Baze said. "There are other goals I'd like to attain. I hope I do get to ride some of those big horses in the big races."

How much more?

"Oh I don't know. Right now, as good as I feel, it's not unreasonable to think I could ride until I'm 50," said Baze, 41. "The hardest part is the injuries, which I really haven't had that many [touch wood], besides that, the dieting, to have to watch the weight all the time."

Why would you stop?

"Either because I'm physically unable to do the job the horses deserve or I'll just get tired of doing it," he said. "I'm sure I will get to an age that it will be difficult to get psyched up and hopefully I'll be smart enough to know when that day comes."

Did you read your Hall of Fame plaque? What did you think of it?

"Yup. I thought it was cool. I don't pay attention to the facts or the statistics or the numbers so I don't really realize all the stuff I've been able to accomplish in my career," Baze said. "When you have it stamped out there in cold steel, it really makes you think, 'I've accomplished some really cool things.' "

How's it feel to be included with the greatest of all time?

"I don't think it's really dawned on me, the full importance of being in there. But it's something they can't take away from me," Baze said. "Eventually I guess I'll realize how important it is."

Have you ever thought about the all-time record for wins? (Baze has over 6,600 career wins; Bill Shoemaker has the record with 8,833 with Laffit Pincay Jr. closing in on it—Pincay would break the record on December 10).

"Everybody out there says you have to catch Shoemaker. I say it's not Shoemaker it's Laffit. I don't think about it. Realistically, I don't think I can keep up the pace we've been setting too much longer," Baze said. "Although I have a heck of an agent who keeps putting me on awful good horses and they keep running their eyeballs out. Another year or two of 400 then hopefully we won't tail off too much."

Sounds like he's thought about it.

What about your son, will he be a jockey?

"He hasn't shown a lot of interest in it, although the other day he said, 'Dad, you got a really cool job.' He's the biggest of the kids, so there is a chance he'll outgrow the occupation anyway."

If he decided to be a jockey would you help him?

"Yeah. I don't know, though, how easy it would be for me to watch him, knowing the hazards that lie in wait out there. I wouldn't relish the idea, put it that way."

Did you go around the Hall of Fame and read the plaques?

"Yeah, had my very own personal tour. I didn't get a chance to read many of them, I read Gary Stevens' because he's on the same wall as I am," Baze said. "I just kinda want to go around and read Arcaro's and some of the other big-name riders and some of the trainers. There's some really interesting stories in there."

Today there's one more: Russell Baze.

CONVERSATIONS
Wednesday, August 11

Writing this from my office on Tuesday night. Figured I'd write instead of eat. Big cup of tea, and a head full of Saratoga.

The yearling sales start tonight. I was thinking about asking *The Backstretch* magazine for a spot of cash so I could buy a yearling. Now that Succeed is a foxhunter, I thought we might need another research project.

Succeed knows a good thing. We tried to ship him home yesterday; he wanted no part of leaving Saratoga, so he's still here. I arrived at the barn to see him in a box stall on the van with a broken halter and a look on his face like "I don't want to go home." I quickly made the decision for him to stay. Horses are so smart—he was alone on the van and would not stand for it. Horses are herd animals: give them company and they'll take you anywhere. So Succeed is back in his stall and I need to arrange another ride home for him.

His retirement is sitting OK with me as long as I don't look at him or think about him. I might give him to a friend or keep him as my pet. One thing I know is if you give something away, make sure the givee knows exactly how you feel about the giveaway. Succeed will have a good life; that makes me smile. His steeplechase career wasn't perfect, but maybe perfection doesn't exist and I'd be better off not looking for it.

As for the story for today, I don't really have one. I thought I would try to give you a notes page from the first two weeks of the meet. The sounds, the conversations, the things overheard. All the stuff that won't quite make a whole story but might add a little color to our lives.

Morning conversation. *(Deirdre Davie)*

This is who I met.

Eddie, a 66-year-old exercise rider who has galloped horses at Saratoga for 52 straight years. I asked him how he ever found the racetrack.

"I lived across the street from Belmont and discovered a world of my own. I was short everywhere else, but there I was even taller than some. I rode a few races but then served in the Korean War; it put some chow on me," Eddie recalled.

He told me about galloping in the good old days on horses like Politely, Gamely, Lamb Chop. He rode Kelso.

"The game was great then, now it's a business. I don't like it anymore. I still love animals—the horses. I can never get away from them."

Eddie was riding Nunzio, a Holy Bull 2-year-old, for Leo O'Brien. He noticed that the horse wouldn't walk into the puddle yesterday and did today. Noticed that "nothing backs him off."

Eddie is a real-life hero. The whole interview process was done on horseback and he doesn't even know I'm a writer, that's one of the reasons I don't know his last name. Did you ever meet someone who puts your heart in line, like a goodness check? Eddie set me right for the day.

Jose Beitia, a 21-year-old jockey from Panama. Jose came by the O'Brien barn looking for rides. If you ever want a shot, come by Barn 61, they'll give you a chance. Ask Barry the hotwalker or Ramon the groom. Jose jumped on You'll Be Happy and we went for a ride. Mr. O'Brien told us to gallop three times around Clare Court, the small track under the trees. So off we went. As we reached the track, Jose looked at me and asked, "I work three-eighths with you?"

"No, no. We're going three times around Clare Court."

"Eh?"

"Just follow me." (Said with sign language, the old head toss to the back and hand behind hand signal.)

I think of how massive and all-encompassing Saratoga is to me. I've been coming here my whole life, I speak the language, it's familiar to me and it still scares me. Saratoga has the ability to overwhelm at any moment. Here's Jose, lost and trying to make a name for himself while he can't even understand what is being said. Nice kid, though. Now I sound old, calling him a kid.

On our way back from Clare Court, I asked him why he came here.

He said yes. And I said no. And he looked at me puzzled. A friend of his rode past, or at least an interpreter for the moment. I asked him to ask Jose why he came here.

The interpreter just looked at me, without asking Jose. "To do better, like all of us."

The interpreter was from Panama, too. Made me think about what we don't think about in our average day, the chance to do better.

Jose has ridden a handful of races so far. I'm rooting for him to win one at Saratoga because—in his words—Saratoga is the best.

Dave. Dave is a young kid who parks cars for a living. He's 16 and goes to work in the parking lot between Union Avenue and Horse Haven. The day I met him, he was standing in the heat of the sun, with an orange traffic director's flag as entertainment. I asked him one question.

"If you could have three things what would they be?"

Without hesitation he said, "A car, more money and a chick."

I laughed. "I was thinking a chair, a book and some shade."

He looked at me with 16-year-old eyes. "I'm thinking long-term, man."

A couple of days later, Dave sat on a sawhorse, flag at his feet. "You know that chair and book would look pretty good right about now," he said.

Here's some worth repeatings.

Trainers Leo O'Brien and Gary Sciacca having a conversation with three jocks' agents over one race.

Gary: "Leo why do you always give firewater to the Indians?"

Leo: "I didn't know they were the Indians."

Owner John Peace standing under a tree in the paddock.

"People live another year for one more Saratoga."

Small child to Jerry Bailey on the way to the paddock.

"Can you sign it 'Happy Birthday, Jim.'"

Bailey: "Happy Birthday, Jim? That'll be extra."

He laughed, she looked horrified—until he signed it.

And here's one more from the e-mail file.

About Succeed: "Whatever he does, I'm sure he'll do it with class."

I ride Pinkie Swear in the first on Wednesday and Welcome Parade on Thursday. Working on getting this duck out of my life. (If you get blanked at Saratoga, they say you got a duck. I have a whole flock from years past and I don't need another.)

So that's all from here—nearly seven now, need to shower, shave, eat (a little) and buy that yearling for *The Backstretch*. What should we name him?

Writer's Block. At The Spa. Succeed Again. Inthebook. Saratoga Days.

IN THE PINK

Thursday, August 12

Where do I begin? I just came home from the sales, the home of the $6 drink. It's a little after eleven and I'm teetering between total exultation and total exhaustion. I was greeted by 36 e-mails, thanks to all of you (I mean that). Every time I hear that you enjoy what I'm doing, it picks me up. I'll answer as soon as I can.

I don't need picking up tonight. The duck is gone. Pinkie Swear became my fifth career Saratoga winner. I even did what I asked Pat Johnson to do. I'll tell you, in all my life, there is nothing like galloping back to the wire and facing your horse to the Saratoga infield. I took it in. And it was something.

An absolutely amazing day. Sorry, I'm exhausted and need to go to bed. I can't do it justice tonight, so I'll try tomorrow. Bear with me.

I'm back. It's Thursday morning, a little after seven. I decided against galloping horses again this morning. This book project has my exercise rider career in jeopardy, thank God. I miss the horses but I don't miss the wake-up call.

I met Pinkie Swear in the fall of 1997. I schooled and galloped him before his first start. I gave him a bad ride in his debut over jumps and he fell. That was the last time I rode him until yesterday. He was sold after his first start—to Charlie Fenwick, a trainer I don't ride for very often. I hadn't ridden a race for him in years.

So anyway, I received a note last Saturday night/Sunday morning from Fenwick about riding my old friend Pinkie. To be honest, he is a horse that I've been watching for a long time. Jockeys see the occasional horse they think they can change something on or improve enough to make a difference. Pinkie was a little this way. Just a couple of nudges, a couple of pulls—and maybe a second place becomes a victory. Sometimes it works, sometimes it doesn't.

I always thought that Pinkie needed a positive and inspired ride from his jockey. For him to win, he could not get in any traffic and the jockey could never give up on him. He lost some races that I thought he could have won if he had a smoother trip and if he had a more aggressive ride at the end. You couldn't let Pinkie think he was tired. I wanted to convince Pinkie that there was more to give and once he gave it, that he would be happy about giving it. I wasn't sure if I could make a difference, but I was sure psyched to try.

So Pinkie and I got back together. Well nearly. We jumped the first four fences well, then the fifth was approaching.

He had been standing off (lifting off the ground early) at his fences, but not that confidently, so I decided to perch up his neck and give him a squeeze, which was supposed to give him confidence. I perched and asked him to leave the ground but he missed my cue and dove right into the fence. I lost my reins, my left stirrup, and about two lengths. It's a wild feeling, when you're about to fall off and then even wilder when you don't. So with that mess out of the way, we set off (with a major confidence issue) for six more fences.

Sometimes, horses (and jockeys) lose their confidence after a mistake like that, but not this time. He came to the next fence and jumped it perfectly, which helped our nerve.

Heading down the backside, I was on the inside, still going well but maybe not as well as favorite Muscle Car. He looked like he was cruising and I had already started on the reserve. Horses were ranging up all over the place. Around the turn I was all out, which

Pinkie Swear turns toward the crowd (check out the payoffs). *(Elizabeth Hendriks)*

usually will only get you tired, but Pinkie kept digging. He didn't lose any ground and I kept thinking about getting up the inside in the stretch.

As we turned for home, I implored Pinkie for one more furlong—for the good of the journal, for my readers, for my dad down in Pennsylvania watching on simulcast—one more furlong, old boy. He shot up the inside of Assurance, made a huge leap at the last (Hokan!) and held off the favored entry of Muscle Car and Invest West.

Coming down the lane, after we made the lead, was a battle with my head and body. I was getting tired and so was Pinkie, but we couldn't give up. I also wanted to savor it at the same time. I just tried to keep a rhythm, the same motion. Trying to get to the line first at Saratoga will make your insides split.

I could win a hundred races anywhere else and it doesn't compare to winning one here.

As a writer, I can't seem to give it what it deserves. It is of such magnitude that words seem to pale in comparison.

I want to write this glorious Red Smith column about Pinkie Swear and it seems like it's just me talking about a horse. Where's Red when you need him?

Back at it today on Welcome Parade in the first. Now if I could win this one, maybe Red Smith will appear. Tonight we'll be back at the sales—find me at the bar along with Rick Pitino and the rest of the movers and shakers.

The sales are out of my league. It just doesn't seem like real money. $1.35 million for a horse. She was cute, a filly by Kingmambo, but $1.35 million? Money, it's an amazing thing.

Yesterday, I walked into the sales pavilion, nodded at a couple of people and watched the spotters (men in tuxedos who "spot" the bids), listened to the auctioneer, took a couple of pictures. Then I went to the bar, to my crowd, and ended up in 10 conversations at once.

I'm still waiting for *The Backstretch* to wire me that money for our yearling. Psst, I'll settle for beer money.

MONEY FOR NOTHING

Friday, August 13

Meet Hip 186. A son of Mr. Prospector and the Cox's Ridge mare Eaves. Big. Bay. Great eye. The Three Million Dollar Horse.

The most expensive Saratoga yearling purchase since 1984 was resting after a harried week at the Spa while the shorts and T-shirt crowd swarmed his stall.

"Just wanted a glimpse."

"He's the king today."

"He looks like a such a gentle spirit. I know he's supposed to be aggressive and run, but he's so peaceful."

The bay colt just packed the Humphrey S. Finney sales pavilion and stopped the gavel at a cool three million. That's right, $3 million for a horse. The gawking still wouldn't stop.

He finally flopped down in his straw and called it a day, while Taylor Made Sales Agency's general manager, Frank Taylor, walked laps around the courtyard in front of the sales topper. On a cell phone, drink in hand, Taylor couldn't stop talking. He had the colt's new owner, Aaron Jones, the man who just spent $3 million for his horse, on the line. Taylor looked like a cross between a new father, a television evangelist and a lottery winner.

He was in the zone, bragging about the colt. A dozen times he repeated, "He's awesome. He's the best I've ever seen."

Enough said. Taylor darted from the horse's stall to his chair to his feet and back to the stall. Great place to be a spectator, standing under a tree, watching fans stop at the king's stall, listening to Taylor and dreaming about what $3 million would do for your life.

The sales are so addicting because of horses like this one. Knowing there won't be many more Mr. Prospectors (the brilliant sire died on June 1) to follow into the ring. It's history happening.

Bubba and his $3 million body. *(Barbara D. Livingston)*

Wander up to the horse's stall and watch him sigh, eat, sleep.

The money is incomprehensible. The horse is a horse.

The pavilion was packed as he walked into the ring tonight. His pedigree page jumped out of the catalogue like an Armani suit at K mart. Every seat in the house had a body in it waiting to see the cash flow. Fans stood six deep all the way around the balcony to see $3 million spent for a horse. I could hear the horse's heartbeat.

The bidding went like lightning, past $1 million, $2 million, and eventually stalled at $3 million. The bids came from outside, but the pavilion was still hushed as the sold sign went up.

Exhale—I realized I hadn't breathed since the horse went into the ring—and then applause. It just doesn't seem like the same money we spend to put gas in the car or groceries in the cabinets.

My $450 on payday still looks like a lot of cash to me.

Taylor finally says farewell to Jones—with yet another "He's the best I've ever seen"—and eventually Barn 7B settles down and the showstopper finally gets some rest. Taylor tells the night watchman to guard that stall, So the lights go out, Taylor heads to Siro's, and the $3 million baby goes to bed.

He's worth $3 million and he doesn't even know it.

I head back to the bar, where the world talks about Hip 186. I hear conversations like this:

"I'm going home."

"Home? There's no going home in this town. This is the wildest town I've ever been to."

The man who said "home" follows the man who said "home?" to Siro's, and bedtime is postponed for another day.

And the beat goes on. To the Parting Glass for our project—I finished my research a little after three. The bartender told us, "Come on guys, we'd like to go home."

So we went home. Woke up this morning and went to visit "Bubba." He doesn't have a name yet, but his catalog number, Hip 186, just won't do. He looks like a Bubba. Just checked to see if he turned into $3 million yet. He's a good-looking horse, intelligent, but he still looks like a horse to me. I wonder what a pile of three million $1 bills would look like in that room of straw. Horses don't even know what they're worth. Maybe that's why they're so easy to get along with.

Bubba reminds me of Succeed in a way. In a big-bay-with-a-great-eye kind of a way. I hope someone takes his time with Bubba and that he conjures up the same Succeed feelings I felt. Maybe Bubba will make the sequel to this book, Saratoga Days II—a day-to-day journey through Saratoga 2000.

I managed to get some good photos of Bubba leaving Saratoga. I waited outside his stall—good thing I quit my galloping job—until the Sallee horse van was ready for its trip to Kentucky. Cordell and Snake, the men in charge of the big horse, put a pair of bell boots on Bubba's front feet and led the $3 million horse to the loading chute.

Snake and Cordell laughed about handling such an expensive animal and then coddled him like a newborn. I stood there and watched this massive yearling walk onto the horse van and wondered about the world. $3 million for a horse.

DANCE
Saturday, August 14

"If you'll be my Dixie chicken, I'll be your Tennessee lamb and we can walk together down in Dixieland . . ."

Come dance with me. I'll sing in your ear. You might have to lead. And I can't follow a beat, but come on and dance.

Until you dance the Dixie Chicken at Siro's, Saratoga is just another town. Little Feat on the piano, at two in the morning—make your way for the dance floor.

Saratoga was at its best last night. I made my annual pilgrimage to the Hall of Fame Ball. Once a year, I put on my costume (tuxedo) and dance to Lester Lanin. I decided against the digital camera, seemed a little tacky to start shooting photos of Marylou Whitney. So envision me with the rest of the aristocrats, black tie and glittery dresses, at the Gideon Putnam Hotel.

Trainer Gary Sciacca told me last year at the ball, "If you ever see me at one of these things again, shoot me." Next time you see Sciacca in the paddock, think about him knotted up in black tie trying to make small talk with the Queen of England.

I find the ball entertaining. Great place to people watch and to find a new perspective. One woman in a long white dress went wading in the kiddie pool. There she was, dress hiked up to her waist, standing in two feet of water. Hell, it was hot.

The rest of us were on our best behavior. At least until we relocated to Siro's, the bar right next to the track. That's when the Dixie Chicken came back to Saratoga. Every year, I have (at least) one wild night at Siro's. Not sure how I got there or how I'll get out, but I'm there.

This one song sends me flying every year. I heard the first few notes from the piano last night, grabbed trainer Kathy Neilson, and cleared the dance floor. In an instant, we went from drink-in-hand conversation to a runaway night. The bar room became the dance floor in one verse.

This is Saratoga—when you're up late and so absolutely alive. Dancing, singing, laughing, but most of all just taking a moment to

Siro's, land of enchantment. *(Harlan Marks)*

let it out. That's the best part of Saratoga, those moments when you howl at the moon.

We howled and flew to the moon last night. Danced in and out of the craters.

Today, it's reality. Trying to protect our world, put out fires, take care of friends. That's why we relish nights like last night. Reality waits. We yawp, strut, carouse, and put off the real world. The next day the real world comes back; it always does. We aren't any better at handling it, maybe worse, but we still had a few moments where the fence was up and reality was on the other side.

Inevitably, the fence is gone in the morning.

Saratoga brings that to the front. This isn't the safety and comfort of home. It's out in the open. No blankets, no crutches, no routines. Saratoga can change your life forever. Coming to Saratoga for the season is like stepping into a fantasy. No one leaves Saratoga the same as they arrived.

Moments of pure release. And moments of pure suffocation. It's all about how you deal with them.

Adversity. Tragedy. Despair. They come to Saratoga. It's a majestic place but it can't escape those strikes. Saratoga can beat them, however. They exist, but the quality of life here wins out. Not money or fame. It's mind frame and attitude. Air and water. Porches and mountains. Horses and restaurants. Mornings and nights. Locals and tourists.

All hell could break loose here and still Saratoga would rise above.

MEET THE STARS

Sunday, August 15

Do you know the difference between horses and Ping-Pong balls? Horses and dice? Horses and silver scratch-off circles?

Horses have personalities. Likes. Dislikes. Moods. Traits. Senses of humor. Habits. Emotions. Friends. Houses. Families. Routines. Eyes. Ears. Tails. Tales. Charisma. Bravery. Fears. Good days. Bad days. Off days. Days off. Senses. Heartbeats.

"You need to meet me,"
Honor Glide.
(*Barbara D. Livingston*)

And you need to know about them all. You need to meet the horses. Come to the barn, see them in their element. See how they relax. See how they react. See how they sleep. When you do, when you begin an attachment, you are a fan. Forever.

Horse racing needs fans. That is a certainty. If you're reading this, you are already a fan. But why? You certainly have a story. Maybe it's your upbringing. Dad take you to the track? Maybe your interest in the horse. Did you have a pony? Maybe your neighborhood. Did you live outside the stable gate? Some hook. Some reason you are here. The desire to follow the game is in you.

That's what needs to be created in the rest of the world. People on the inside can't figure out why the average person doesn't flock to see the horses run. We can't see it because we're already here.

I stopped by Christophe Clement's barn this morning to check on Honor Glide, runaway winner of yesterday's Sword Dancer. Now I know him. Now I will follow his every move. Now I will recognize him in the morning.

I now know Honor Glide. Clement's assistants, mostly of French descent, told me about his last workout—"Everybody came back smiling." Told me about the way he is around the barn—"You could applause [remember, they're French] and it wouldn't bother him." They offered me doughnuts. They asked me what Honor Glide would be like to ride over jumps (I asked them to let me find out). They were proud of their horse.

Honor Glide, as Clement put it, is "not too social this morning." In the stall right next to the tack room, Honor Glide didn't have much need for me. I walked to his stall and said hello; he turned and poked his head out over his webbing. Tried to bite me and went back to what he was doing before. A cross between sleeping and ignoring. Eventually he came out and looked around at the fuss. Tried to bite some passersby and pinned his ears. He's not vicious, just not very social.

You need to see this. Well, maybe you don't, because if you're reading, you are probably a major racing fan. But the fringe, that's who needs to see this part of this world. The fringe fans. They need a story to follow. Once you get to know a horse, you can watch for him, go to the races when he runs, bet on him, have a direct link to the sport. I knew about Honor Glide before this morning. But now I know him.

The horse is the best prospect of landing that hook, but trainers, jockeys and owners will do, too. I galloped horses back in 1994 with Jose Valdivia Jr. at P. G. Johnson's stable. We became friends. He was a 10-pound apprentice jockey, trying to get a break. I was a 24-year-

Honor Glide rolls away the morning. *(Barbara D. Livingston)*

old steeplechase jockey trying to win my first race at Saratoga. Now he follows my career and I follow his. I guess I made it in my field. So has he. Valdivia won three Grade II stakes on Big Jag earlier this year, and their sights are set on the Breeders' Cup. I look for Big Jag and root for Big Jag, strictly because I met Jose Valdivia Jr. five years ago.

It isn't that easy to get to know the players in horse racing. But it should be. I'm talking to racetrack management and horsemen—we better welcome this concept before it's too late. Fans demand it. You want to know the stories that go along with every horse and every horseman.

Saratoga is good at it, at least comparatively speaking. Breakfast at the track. Stable tours. The jockeys still walk through the crowd at the races. Horses come as close to fans here as anywhere in the world. And, voila, Saratoga is the Mecca for horse racing.

Obviously, breakfast at the track, guided tours and a meet and greet with the horses won't turn Aqueduct into Saratoga. But a day at Saratoga, when a connection to the sport is made, might keep you out of the casinos and at the racetrack.

Anybody can read about a $3 million colt. But walk up to his stall, listen to him sigh, see him get scared by the clatter at the breakfast counter, walk with him to the horse van—in person or along with me—and you will feel a connection.

He'll be unforgettable now. He won't be just another horse. He'll be a horse you know.

LOOSE LEGENDS

Monday, August 16

What do you think of this brainstorm?

We all get together. We could have our own roundtable about racing and Saratoga. I'm thinking, just for fun, we could all meet and talk about what's on our minds. No soapboxes, no attitudes.

Bring something. A story. A book. A question. Just contribute to the gathering. Beer. Crackers. Chairs. Anything at all. It would be cool if everyone brought a passage to read.

I would like to read "Saratoga, or The Horse at Home," by Joe H. Palmer. My friend Bill gave me the *Fireside book of Horse Racing* when I did the seminar before the meet opened. An incredible collection of racing stories written by some of the greatest writers of all time: Palmer, Granny Rice, Red Smith, Damon Runyon; the book will blow you away.

If you ever looked at a horse or a horse race with a hint of curiosity then this book will engulf you.

I'm picturing a bunch of us in Congress Park, some refreshments and some readings. Tell me what you think. If we find an array of responses then we'll give it a try. I thought of this because of the last race today.

A bad bunch of off-the-turf fillies. But no matter the quality of the field, the bettors yell. The race was so desperate (my ticket was worthless at the half-mile pole) that I started watching the crowd.

"Come onnnn BABY . . . " was the loudest of all. So I took a picture. With a digital camera, you can see your photo as soon as your finger comes off the button. Right under the yeller is a women with her fingers in her ears. It was the perfect racetrack moment. One bettor trying to get home and one fan trying to get home with the hearing she came with. Not sure which one was successful although the "Come onnnn BABY . . . " diminished around the eighth-pole, which usually means BABY stopped. I had a good laugh when I looked at the picture. It was so funny I had to show her. She laughed and we started talking. She asked me why I was taking pictures. I said I write a column on the internet. She said, "You're Sean?"

Hello Susan. So, yeah, I met Susan, a reader. She offered Succeed a lifelong home. We talked for a while. As a writer you don't get to meet too many of the people who read your daily thoughts. I thought a gathering might be fun and possibly useful. As much as I hate criticism it might do me good to sit around and listen to what the readers want. So that's what made me think about our own group session. Nothing strict or formal, just something to do; maybe we'd all learn something.

So, again, let me know what you think.

As for the life and times of Saratoga. The old man came to check on us. Fourstardave is back where he belongs. He looks older but still spry and alert. I haven't seen Dave since last year up here. He didn't miss me. Dave is aloof. He likes to see what you're up to but as far as any attention or affection, forget it. Just a loner in an honest way.

Fourstardave—not loose. *(Barbara D. Livingston)*

For eight consecutive years, Fourstardave was Saratoga. Well, he still is in a historical way, but from 1987 to 1994, Dave won a race at Saratoga for owner Richard Bomze and trainer Leo O'Brien. This will never be done again. Horses just don't last that long or stay that good. Dave stayed genuine and fast for eight straight years. They called him the Sultan of Saratoga.

Since I was friends with the O'Briens and worked for them over the years, Dave became a family member. Well, he's like a big brother who rips me every day. I'll say it here: I was afraid of Dave. And he knew it.

I've held this story for an occasion like this. About halfway through his streak, I was working for the O'Briens when Leo decided I needed to learn how to be a pony boy. This is when you ride the lead pony and take a racehorse with you for exercise. A leather shank with about three feet of light brass chain around the racehorse's nose is about the extent of the control. Horses are amazing creatures—they really don't know how easily they could get away from the human touch if they wanted. Well, Dave knew.

"Sean, you want to jump on the pony for this set," Leo said.

Sure.

"I'll give you Dave, you can wander around."

Uh, Mr. O'Brien, I've never ponied a horse in my life.

"Ah, what a way to learn."

So Dave and I became instant brothers. He being the Big Brother with a menacing sense of humor and me the defenseless baby brother.

We went out for wanders every day. He had already won his race for the meet, so he was having a little rest—he wouldn't run again until Belmont. No galloping or working, mostly wandering for a couple of weeks. And they wonder how the horse stayed so competitive for so long. It was the wandering. And the winters off, but that's another book.

So Dave and I would mill around the backstretch, jog a little here and there on the Oklahoma track, stop and socialize with other barns. It was terrifying. Every person knew it was Fourstardave. Here was the Saratoga legend, who absolutely knew it, and me. I felt like a giant bullseye, and Dave had the darts. He would torment my pony and me day after day. He loved it. Finally the pony, whose name I can't remember, had enough. Dave would reach over and grab him by the withers (the high part of his back, right where the saddle sits) and shake him like an upside-down piggy bank. All for fun.

The last day I ponied him, and you'll see why it was the last day, we started onto the Oklahoma track by Shug McGaughey's barn. Dave leapt up in the air and came down with his mouth squarely around the pony. That was it: the most patient creature in the world (the universal lead pony) couldn't take it anymore. He bucked and kicked out at Dave.

This was like spitting on the president. Dave jumped away and looked at us like, "that ain't part of the game." When Dave jumped, the pony jumped and the leather shank slid to the tip of my fingers. I was leaning off my pony with about eight feet between Dave and me and about a thumbnail of shank in grip. This was like dropping both hands in the ring with Ali. Dave looked me right in the eye and tossed his head. The shank went from my hand to the dirt. Fourstardave was loose. And I had done it. A loose horse is the most dangerous and harrowing thing on the racetrack, a loose Fourstardave . . . this was the most dangerous and harrowing thing in my lifetime.

There's Fourstardave standing in the middle of the Oklahoma track looking at me, free as a bird. But he just stood there. Most horses cut. You don't know which way they went. Dave just looked me in the eye. Horses were galloping past on either side. And there's Dave. I finally acted, and gave my pony a nudge to walk over. I got within a hand of the shank and Dave turned his head and walked away.

Horses are delicate animals, especially when they're loose. You can't just tackle them. Any sudden movement will backfire the whole "catch him" process.

Dave let me walk up to him five times and each time he just turned and ambled away, never even jogging, just walking and looking over his shoulder to see if I was still playing his game. I had no choice.

On the sixth attempt, I got reinforcements. James Bond, the trainer of Behrens, was watching the scene from the rail. He looked at me and I looked at him; no words were spoken. He started walking from the other side as I started walking from my side, two grown men trying to outsmart one horse. Like defusing a bomb. When I got within a hand, Dave turned away from me, right into Bond's outstretched hand. Dave didn't mind being caught, it was just a game anyway. Bond handed me the shank. We managed to stay off the front page of the *Form* and I still had a job.

Dave never put a foot wrong the rest of the day. We cantered once around and walked home without a sound.

Dave was simply entertaining himself. When he got loose, that really wasn't the game he wanted to play. He was playing mess with the kid, not get loose and run all over Saratoga. He played the game better than anyone.

Like Mr. O'Brien said, what a way to learn. And Mr. O'Brien, I'm sorry I never told you this story, but as they say, what you don't know won't hurt you.

What else, you ask?

Today, Jerry Bailey did it in plain view. Right there for all to see. He put Pleasant Temper on the lead in the Ballston Spa Breeders' Cup and stole a $200,000 purse.

Bailey is amazing. I root for the low man, but Bailey deserves all the accolades. He rides nothing but favorites but never seems to leave the race in doubt. If I was a jockey doing badly, I would see where Bailey is at all times and emulate him. I would track him, dog him, chase him. Can't figure out what to do? Do the next best thing, be Bailey. He's on a horse with a chance and he rides a smart race, so why not be next to him? If you were driving down the highway and Jeff Gordon pulled up next to you, wouldn't you follow him? Just wondering. That's what I would do—if in doubt, find Bailey and do what he does. Even after the races.

I listened to a school of children pester Bailey for autographs and goggles as he walked from the track to the jocks' room after the race. He told them to meet him in the back by the scales. Twenty minutes later Bailey, showered and dressed, signed every autograph and gave away a trunk full of goggles. The kids went crazy. On behalf of Thoroughbred racing, thanks, Jerry, and all the other jockeys who take the time. Good move. Those kids will now grow up to be die-hard racing fans.

Speaking of die-hard racing fans. Today was beer stein giveaway. They ran out. People walked around the track with cases of steins, broken steins, purchased steins. They were everywhere, and the place was packed. I leaned against a post and listened to the crowd.

"We saved two bucks but walked an extra 18 miles."

"Thirty thousand six hundred and fifty dollars. I got the fifty but . . ."

"Go around. You can go around. What are you, stupid?"

"Lenny, is this still on the turf?" "It was never on the turf, Joe."

"Go inside or outside."

We went home.

IN LOVE AGAIN

Tuesday, August 17

Halftime at Saratoga. The dark Tuesday between the first three weeks and the last three weeks.

I never in my life realized how significant the dark day is to one's mental stability. In this life, it has become my one-day weekend. It's not even a whole day, just an afternoon without any racing. I still woke up with the crickets this morning, but at least I found a short respite. I used to hate dark days; that was before this project. Of course, Saratoga conveniently crams in another horse sale to nix your afternoon nap.

I happened to see yet another majestic creature. Hip 650. Did you ever hear horsemen say a horse has presence? This one has Lady Di presence.

She's a tall daughter of Summer Squall. I think I'll buy her this afternoon. Put it on the expense account. I'm accepting applications for syndicate members.

It's an amazing side to horses. If you ever bought a horse, you will buy another. Understand? After Succeed, I said I would never take on another horse project. And I actually thought I wouldn't want to.

She's here somewhere. *(Deirdre Davie)*

No more Riverdees, Andrew Sans, Striking Norths. I wanted to end with Succeed. He was the best and a good one to stop on. Then I turn the corner of Horse Haven, aboard Leo O'Brien's lead pony Snowball, and see the massive bay body—and the presence. I file her number, 650, and head out to the Oklahoma with Keith O'Brien on Critics Acclaim. The wild thing about living with horses is that Keith and I oooh'd at the exact same time. We were running our mouths when we turned the corner and she greeted us. We both went silent and stared. Wow, to be exact. Cindy Crawford couldn't have stunned us more.

So this morning, I bolted out of the barn to see my new favorite horse breeze for the sales. I sat there for an hour watching numbers pass on the track when I realized I was supposed to be on a telephone interview with the racing network TVG at noon. I had 15 minutes. So I sprinted down to the paddock and met my Cindy Crawford. She was about to breeze and looked agitated for having to wait. The presence is still there. So that was that. I did my Michael Johnson to the car and came home to do the interview.

Now my banker is working on wiring the money. Damn, I wish I was rich.

Maybe we'll follow her career. I'll go over and watch her sell this afternoon and let you know if we get outbid.

The interview went OK—one of those things I do when I'm asked. Figure it's good practice, for what I don't know. Gave out the address so maybe we'll pick up some more roundtable members.

Sometimes this everyday column is mind-boggling. The amount of material (i.e. stories) I can't even touch upon would blow you away. I still haven't mentioned champion Countess Diana winning her comeback, jockey Edgar Prado cracking the top five in his first Saratoga season, Richard Migliore, the man Prado replaced, spectating, jump jockey Gus Brown winning his first race at Saratoga. This place is a town of stories. Getting to them is the chore.

I still want to meet the kid who was dragged out of the starting gate earlier in the meet. Spend a morning at Dunkin' Donuts. Escape to Lyrical Ballad, the used-book store on Phila Street. Steal the Travers Canoe. Spend an afternoon with Chuck Simon and Allen Jerkens. This town is too big for one pen.

$\mathscr{D}$rift $\mathscr{A}$way

 On our dark day we read. Here's my selected reading for our round table in the park.

"Saratoga, or The Horse at Home" by Joe H. Palmer.

American racing was seriously disrupted about ninety years ago by a dispute over states' rights. The war which accompanied this ended calamitously through the hasty action of a General R. E. Lee at Appomattox, presumably because he did not then envision Paul Robeson, but racing gained here, as it does in most wars. It got Saratoga.

In 1863, with the southern tracks such as Metarie and Lexington slightly unavailable because of the growth of paternalism in the Federal government, a group of racing men staged a meeting at Saratoga, which had long been a health resort in the days before you could keep your health by buying pills or choosing the proper brand of cigarettes. If my information is correct, there was corn growing in the infield, foreshadowing the corn which is still connected with Saratoga. But a lot of people, including this typist, like corn.

The meeting was so surprisingly successful that a somewhat better site was picked out and a grandstand constructed for a meeting in 1864. There still exists, in the spidery handwriting of one of the long dead Alexanders of Woodburn, a list of the nominations which that nursery made to the first running of the Travers Stakes of

1864. One of them, a three-year-old named Kentucky, won it, running a mile and three-quarters in 3:18¾, because this was before stop watches caught time in fifths of a second.

There is a temptation here to write about Kentucky, but it will be resisted. But the notation has to be made that in 1861 the stallion Lexington, referred to in the somewhat sentimental periodicals of the day as the "Blind Hero of Woodburn," got three foals—Kentucky, Norfolk, and Asteroid—which left the races as "the Great Triumvirate." None of the three was ever beaten, except on the one occasion that two of them met in the same race.

If you will look through the records of yesteryear, you will find that the Travers Stakes was run in 1897 and was not run again until 1901, and that there is an even longer lacuna in the history of the Saratoga Cup at about the same time. The reason is that in the late '90s Saratoga fell flat on its face, and that before the 1901 meeting a group of prominent racing owners headed by W. C. Whitney (grandfather of C. V. Whitney and Greentree Stable) picked it up and set it to running again. The Grand Union Hotel Stakes, the Saratoga Special, the Saratoga Handicap and the Albany Handicap date from that year, the latter race being so named before it was realized that this was feeding the hand that bites you. The Hopeful was instituted then, although, being a futurity, it was not run until 1903.

What W. C. Whitney and his friends understood in 1901 is still apparent to the more serious minds in racing. A fresh deck has been substituted since. Even when this tourist first went to Saratoga there were six races a day, starting at two-thirty or three (memory wavers a little), and people were out of the track at five o'clock to begin tanking up against the yearling sales which followed after dinner. Now it's eight races and the daily double and the

The old days. *(Winants Brothers)*

damned public-address system. But Saratoga is still the focal point of racing in New York, at least, and if it goes, something dies.

It used to be that a New York stable could race in Saratoga in August or it could go to hell. Now it can race in Saratoga or it can go to New Jersey or Chicago. This circumstance supplies an excellent touchstone for picking out sheep from goats. The big stables, and the little ones which are honestly interested in the perpetuation of racing, go to Saratoga. They meet, deliberately, tougher competition for a smaller amount of money.

This is because Saratoga, in our time, has become a symbol. It doesn't draw as many people as Jamaica or Aqueduct. It doesn't contribute as much to the state treasury because the handle is lower than at the least of the metropolitan tracks. It has a somewhat antiquated clubhouse from which you cannot see very well unless you have a box or a friend who has one. It doesn't make any money for the stockholders.

Even so, any time you want to know whether racing in New York can still consider itself a sport or whether it is a highly elaborate pin-ball machine, just look to see if Saratoga has dates. There is no objection here to people who try to make money—I try it myself, with rather indifferent success. But there should be, in racing or baseball or business, an occasional gesture which is not made solely toward the cashier.

Now, local horse players are divided, like Gaul, into three parts. Those suffering from severe wounds or extreme battle fatigue will stay at home, get their business in order again, catch up on their correspondence, and note with pleasure how much little Lucy has grown since April 1. Those who have been only slightly scratched will adventure into New Jersey to face the lighter weapons of Atlantic City, a locality which has always beckoned insistently to strong men and weak women. But the Palace

Guard goes to Saratoga, where there is grass on the turf.

When this department was first learning that two and two can be made to equal $9.60 and $4.20, it was felt in the area drained by Elkhorn Creek that Saratoga was quite a promising youngster, considering that it was a parvenu of 1863, with no ante-bellum tradition at all. But the ancient Lexington track was dismantled years ago, for a slum-clearance project, and the dust which had felt the beat of more than a century of racing hooves is now periodically washed from the faces of slightly underprivileged children.

With that dismantling, Saratoga became the oldest of American race tracks, and succeeded legitimately to title of Queen Mother of Racing in these states. She is, as the aged frequently are, somewhat dependent on the loyalty of her children, but this has not ever failed. As yet there are, to be sure, some who deny her authority, now that the old lady has gone into trade to sustain her social position. These may be distinguished in battle by a solid black bar on the left side of their shields.

It is admitted that age and tradition, so becoming to a race track, can be overdone in a hotel, and these remarks are to be applied to Saratoga, the race track, and not without reservation to Saratoga, the village in the foothills of the Adirondacks. There are areas in which the possibilities of indoor plumbing have not been fully explored, and a man may easily feel his enthusiasm vanish when there is a battered washbowl on the bedroom wall and the bathroom's down the corridor and turn to the left.

As to the native fauna of the place, no August visitor can very well testify because there are none at that time. There are, of course, persons who, having made fortunes elsewhere, have made their homes in Saratoga to spend their declining years standing off the natives. But your true Saratogian rents his house, often for less than half the purchase price, in August and goes to live with relatives.

The casinos and roadhouses are operated by outside talent, as is the race track. The reason for this is that, though it is against probability, a man can in theory win either at horse playing or roulette, and the native Saratogian looks upon such a situation as wasteful. A cut of the gross, he reasons, is five times better business.

And yet, one comes to believe on slow, serene, cool mornings that Saratoga does give full value received. If the visitor gets banged about a little, he must remember that for eleven months of the year someone has to work to keep the place in order, to keep the lawns in a level green glow which apparently does not exist anywhere else, and to hold the shrubbery in some sort of order, and for such services, of course, one pays.

I suspect that if all the things one criticizes were promptly remedied, Saratoga would become a modern humdrum town with a race track on the outskirts. Perhaps nothing is as hard to do, or as expensive, as to keep time from passing, and Saratoga has mastered at least the illusion of this, with the result that racing in August is a jewel.

So this summer visitor seems to have argued himself out of any complaints at all. It is to be hoped that Saratogians will keep to their ways, and that the local paper will, as it did two years ago, see no inconsistency in hoping, editorially, that prices would not be raised against August residents. At the same time it was increasing its street price from five cents to ten.

This is the month in which New York horse players are turned out on grass. After five months of concrete and asphalt and gravel, they may have the lawns of Saratoga to play with. They may even take off their shoes and wriggle their toes in the grass, though the Saratoga Association, which is conservative, will not approve.

Actually, of course, the bite is on at Saratoga just as severely as at Aqueduct, and the art of sucker-trimming has been raised to a level which will thrill the connoisseur. Some of this is in the hands of imported organizations but the natives are adept at it, too, and you begin to wonder if Burgoyne lost the Battle of Saratoga by military maladroitness or if the local taverns and hostelries just sapped his resources.

But being deluded, and even being frisked by the citizenry at Saratoga, is a good deal like eating honey. You will notice that the gentry who kick and bawl about prices and practices at Louisville around Derby time seldom have much to say about fleecing in Saratoga, yet I can assure you that over a distance of ground Louisville couldn't give Saratoga a pound.

This is because Saratoga applies an anesthetic, of tranquil shaded lawns, of big white quiet houses, of a leafy and mellowed antiquity, and morning after morning of golden serenity. By the time the subject revives and discovers what has been done to him, time has slipped past and it isn't news any more. Nothing's as dead as yesterday's newspaper expense account.

For the casual race-goer, Saratoga is about the only place in the East where he can see racing. Elsewhere he merely sees races, which isn't the same thing at all. At Saratoga the mornings are almost as much a part of the show as the afternoons, and since some of the stable area is as open to view as the Pennsylvania Station, a visitor doesn't have to know a man or have a badge to get a pretty fair idea of the entire show.

This department cannot conscientiously indorse any uncivilized nonsense like getting up and watching horses work with the morning mists swirling behind them, and while the wood smoke from under the hot water kettles may be stimulating to brighter-eyed people it always reminds me that it hasn't been long enough since last night. Still, it's worth doing once. You will remember it a long time, and that saves having to do it again.

But for persons less avid for experience, I give you Saratoga at the third set, or the second-cup-of-coffee stage when you can begin to see a little, out of one eye. Breakfast on the clubhouse porch is particularly recommended, if only for that sublime sense of sitting at ease and watching other people work.

Though Saratoga avails itself of a squalling public-address system and an unornamental but quite handy Totalisator in the afternoons, it has nevertheless contrived to stand fairly still while racing became "modern." It is the only track this side of Keeneland where horses are saddled in the open, and where the ordinary racing customer can see enough of a horse to recognize him next time. A little outmoded, a little low on verve, and nearly always faintly patronizing toward the slap-dash ways of its contemporaries, Saratoga has kept on with its quiet ways, and its reward is that a little of the old time yet lingers.

A man who would change it would stir champagne.

The Old Kentucky Association track at Lexington was constructed strictly as an affront to whatever muse presides over architecture. Latonia was set in a depression quite properly known as "Death Valley," because it could get more fiendishly hot there in July than anywhere else in the world. You may love Pimlico to your heart's content but you cannot, on oath, call it pretty, and to get around the plant on a Saturday would make an eel take second thought. And some day I may discover why I like Bowie in late November. Careful thought has thus far failed to adduce any reasons.

It is therefore a relief to feel the attraction of a racing plant which demonstrably deserves it. For four wonderful, sleepy weeks—a small voice, calling itself experience, here says, "You mean sleepless weeks"—racing makes at least a partial return to the unhurried, graceful and leisurely atmosphere in which it was born. This flavor lingers in but a few places and is consequently the more precious.

Saratoga has its critics, of course, but it is customarily shelled from long range. Let a man hang around the place for a while and drink his breakfast from the clubhouse porch and you have no more trouble with him. Saratoga is slightly contagious, though you can't catch it at Jamaica.

There is a story that Lily Langtry once upset Saratoga's slow decorum by appearing publicly in red slippers. She would have to go a little deeper than that now, for I suppose a man can see more curious things going up and down Saratoga's Broadway in the morning than he could see in the same time at the Bronx Zoo. But a man has no business on Broadway in the morning. He ought to be either at the race track or sensibly in bed.

The themes at Saratoga are old friends and young horses, and most of the important racing is devoted to finding out what sort of two-year-olds are about. There are excellent and venerable races for horses above that age, notably the Travers and the Saratoga Cup, but from the Flash Stakes on the opening program to the Hopeful on closing day, the youngsters hold the major portion of the stage. Middleground, to refresh your memory, made most of his reputation there. And, not to go too far back, Bimelech, Whirlaway, Devil Diver and Pavot came to their full stature in the Hopeful.

And, of course, there's the biggest gamble of the horse business in the evenings when the Fasig-Tipton Company offers (as of the preliminary catalog) 437 Thoroughbred yearlings gathered from Kentucky, Virginia, Maryland, New Jersey and elsewhere.

You should be warned, perhaps, that horse auctions

are hypnotic. Couple of years ago a friend of mine, who had no more idea of buying a horse than a steam calliope, and not much more use for one, suddenly heard himself make the successful bid on a brood mare with a foal at foot. He seemed somewhat dazed afterward but his wife was well ahead of him in that respect.

"What will we do with them?" she asked me, with the accumulated sadness of all the daughters of Eve. "We just have a three-room apartment."

There is, in the Saratoga infield, a lake. On this lake floats, and has floated since 1620, a small blue canoe. For some years I have tried to find out why it is there, though being lazy naturally and by personal inclination as well, I have not been very persistent about it. Ask one of the older veterans of Saratoga and he smiles mysteriously and shakes his head silently. This is intended to mean he isn't telling. Actually it means he doesn't know.

One reason I haven't worked more on this is that I've had a hint that there's an Indian legend connected with it. If I could be sure of this I'd give up at once, because the noble savage, whatever his merits, was notably deficient in imagination. When I was in the fourth grade I could tell a better lie than any Indian legend I ever heard.

In my own territory, for instance, every limestone jutting which pushes itself out of the river palisades with a drop as much as fifty feet under it is known as "Lovers' Leap." Grub around and you'll find that an Indian maiden, barred by her family or friends or circumstance from meeting up with a good buck, is supposed to have climbed up on it and hopped off on her head. If half the stories had any foundation, the Indian in Kentucky would have become extinct without waiting for Dan'l Boone. So this canoe thing has to be handled carefully.

Thank you, Mr. Palmer.

If you ever see the *Fireside Book of Horse Racing*, buy it.

Palmer was the racing writer for the *New York Herald Tribune* from 1946 to 1952.

When I think of this jumbled mass of columns becoming anything close to the *Fireside Book of Horse Racing*, I wonder if I'm crazy. Did people like Red Smith and Joe Palmer get up every day with a body full of confidence, just knowing that whatever they wrote would be cherished by all the world? Oh to be Red Smith . . . Charles Schulz . . . Rudyard Kipling . . .

NAKED VIEWS
Wednesday, August 18

This will be short. Rushing as usual on a Wednesday, I need to get to the track to win the first. Dr. Ramsey's my ride today. If you like longshots, he's your horse. But I didn't say he was going to win.

Well, you know, I have good taste. My favorite horse in the sale, World Storm, took all of the money; trainer Niall O'Callaghan put up $120,000 for the gorgeous 2-year-old daughter of Summer Squall. My old girlfriend was right: I have expensive taste and a cheap income. I would have bought World Storm and won the Alabama next year. Now there's a story.

I bet someone that she would win the 2000 Alabama. The Alabama Future Book. We'll see.

The rest of Saratoga is quiet for the most part. We had nine people in our three-bedroom house last night. Our record was set in 1997 when we had 29 house guests during the meet. And that was a two-bedroom place. We're up near 15 this year. The amazing thing is I'm the one who wrote the four-digit rent check and I'm on the couch.

I'll see if I can find a story I can tell this afternoon.

OK, one funny moment before I go. This is the best thing said in Saratoga this year. Last week, I spent an hour or two in the sauna with Jose Santos, Mike Smith, Chip Miller and a couple of other fat

Jose Santos with his clothes on. *(Harlan Marks)*

jockeys. So about seven races later, I'm standing in coat and tie, three deep on the rail of the paddock.

Santos rides out of the paddock and looks down at me, standing in the crowd. With a wide grin, he says, "Hey, didn't I see you naked earlier today?" And then he turns his head and rides on out to the racetrack. The crowd went crazy. The guy next to me turned and asked, "What did he say?" He was holding his daughter. I told him I couldn't say with his daughter listening. Vintage Santos.

OK, I'll be back and in better form later.

MUST BE IN THE FRONT ROW
Thursday, August 19

Dear Mike,

Thanks for the letter. After reading about you and your father, I got to thinking. I could envision you and your 72-year-old dad standing at the eighth-pole straining to see the finish of the race. Your father, who is about to have hip replacement surgery, maybe leaning on the Chipwich cart yearning to see the jockeys stand up at the wire. Wondering what the horses actually do when the race is over, what the jockeys do when the race is over. And then limping back to a wooden bench somewhere inside the grandstand.

I was thinking about this yesterday, so I ventured out of the clubhouse box seats, the ones you can see the finish of every race from, and headed down the racetrack. Out of the clubhouse and into the grandstand, past the Sbarro Pizza stand, past the telethcater, past first aid, past the chowder station, past the arcade, past the battalion of benches, past the boiler room, past what seemed like the whole racetrack. My destination was the other side. I found it.

Way down at the other end of the racetrack, I found a spot on the benches. It was Wednesday so there were plenty of open spots. I sat on a long green bench and, I confess, took a nap. That's how tired I am. Every time I slow down, I fall asleep. When I awoke I sat there and wondered if maybe you were around, you and your father. I never found you. But maybe I did. I met a man named Fred. He told me about coming to Saratoga back in the '30s when the bookies lined the racetrack apron. Told me about betting with the blackboard men run by the mob. Told me about betting a horse at 8-5 and a few minutes later, the same horse would be 3-1 but he was stuck with the 8-5. Fred told me about his home in St. Petersburg, Florida. Where the old people go, he explained. Fred sure was pleasant and I thought about him in the clubhouse, with a coat on and in the boxes with me. Fred would have liked that.

So Mike, the reason I'm writing is to offer you something. Do you and your dad want to join me in the boxes? Maybe one weekday (I

You gotta see this. *(Deirdre Davie)*

don't have that much pull on weekends) we can all get together and see the end of the race. All you have to do is wear a coat, and a tie wouldn't hurt. We can find a box and you can see the other side. I remember you writing that it would be nice for your dad to see the finish line once in his life. Here's your chance. It will make a good story and your dad would, I think, enjoy the show.

Tell me what you think, it's just a thought. After spending the afternoon in the—sorry—cheap seats I know what you mean about standing up all day and never seeing the finish. You can stay inside and watch the television but horse racing was meant for the open eye. The eye and the horse. No TV screen funneling it. Although now we even have TVs in the boxes, which do add to the experience.

We can bring along some binoculars to watch the race live and then sit back and view the replay right there from our seats. What do you say?

Maybe next week. How's Monday sound? We can go to the paddock. Have you ever been inside the paddock? You'll like that. The horses, up close, will amaze you. The other day, two guys were halfway down the path to the paddock when they froze and said to each other, "We can't go in there." I told them to come on. They said they didn't know what they were doing. I said neither do any of us but come in for once in your life and see a Thoroughbred. They listened and were in awe after they arrived. Made me laugh. No drinks, no shorts, no running, no yelling, and the paddock is your playground. Maybe I'll cause a stampede to the paddock, and security will have to buckle down. Maybe you'll be a fan forever. Whoops, there I go again, trying to win fans and influence racing.

So back to you, Mike—name a good day. We'll meet around the paddock and your dad will see horse racing the way it was meant to be seen. He can sit down, see the finish, and cherish the day.

Sincerely, Sean

(I never heard from Mike. They sure missed out.)

CHILD'S PLAY

Friday, August 20

"Sometimes they mistake your kindness for weakness. Every morning I wake up and it feels like a high-heel shoe right here in my chest. It won't go up and it won't go down."

The racetrack is no different than any other spot in the world. The horses add a sense of peacefulness, innocence and solitude, but the people struggle through life like anywhere else. Sometimes you don't notice, sometimes you do. I've been speaking to a woman who works for trainer Joe Orseno. I still don't know her name but we chat whenever our paths cross. Yesterday, she said that to me as she walked out of her barn and I hacked Banjo Man home. She was frustrated by the working conditions, the attitude, the pressure. Yup,

Every day is Wash Day at Saratoga. *(Deirdre Davie)*

Saratoga is still real life. Just made me think about her life and my life.

I get e-mail from readers across the country telling me how lucky I am to be in Saratoga doing what I love. How lucky I am to be spending my day with horses. How lucky I am to be riding and writing. I agree and try to remind myself of that whenever I feel myself slipping. I could complain about finishing second on Devil's Reach yesterday or I could be proud of his effort and mine. I could complain about having to lose 10 pounds in the next week or I could look back and taste the gazpacho and the peach/granola pancakes from Beverly's. I could complain about my schedule or realize that being busy is a good thing. I could complain about the full house this week or recognize the brilliance of my nephews, Ryan and Jack. They are the ones who came up with these points to ponder.

About jockeys: "They are the littlest grown-ups I've ever seen."

About the mineral water at the Big Red Spring: "I didn't spit it out because I didn't want to taste it a second time."

About Robbie Davis: "I met Robbie Davison."

I said, it's Robbie Davis, and Ryan said, "Yeah, Robbie Davison."

Saratoga is a town for kids. Maybe that's why we gravitate here, it's our one chance to get back to our origins. You can wander around like kids again. Sleep in, wreck your bike, lose money, eat ice cream at Ben and Jerry's, stay out too late, eat too much, and laugh through it all. There are excuses here for more than could ever be tolerated at home. Somehow the one word answer, Saratoga, is enough to get away with most anything.

I met a kid named Benjamin the other day in the grandstand. He was riding the racehorse game, mechanical version of the real thing. He could ride, too. He knew when to pump, when to sit, when to hit, and when to stand up and cheer. Turns out he's Benjamin Heller, writer Bill Heller's son. He knew who I was, what I wrote, and how my horse ran earlier in the day.

I asked him if he was going to be a jockey, and he told me, "No, I'm too big. I'm going to be a trainer. Or the world's biggest horse racing expert." He's 10 years old and knows what he wants to be. When do we change? When do we go from knowing all the answers to being scared of the questions?

Benjamin made me laugh when he asked me if I go to the press box. I said no, although I did go there for the first time last week. He told me they have everything there. I thought to myself, yeah but they don't have 10-year-old kids riding mechanical horses and expounding about life without even knowing it.

The other reason I avoid the press box is that I haven't found a horse, much less a story, in there yet. (I think I read that somewhere but it sure does fit.)

Tuesday, I have a story. I volunteered, for the good of the book, to drive in a celebrity harness race. Shane Sellers, Shaun Bridgmohan, Joe Deegan and I will ride in some sort of trotting event. That's about the extent of what I know. I'm supposed to head over to the harness track tomorrow and meet my trainer and my horse. And before you ask, no I've never ridden, driven or whatever you do in or on a harness horse. Might be fun. And I'm thinking no jumps and no weight requirements—sounds good to me. I'll let you know how it goes. Come by Tuesday night for a laugh.

Now I'm off to the races for the Yaddo Stakes today. Champion Silverbulletday comes to Saratoga tomorrow for the Alabama.

THE NEIGHBORHOOD
Saturday, August 21

I can't sleep anymore. I was up last night at two in the morning answering e-mails (if you received an incoherent message, you now know why). Then I woke up, late for work like always, and couldn't function. I staggered to Dunkin' Donuts and slugged a tall coffee. Must be the Saratoga lull. It's when money's low, moods are shaky, and senses are off. You can't get to the dry cleaners for a week and when you do they hold up your credit card. Sharon Cleaners, over by Five Points, they clean clothes and find lost VISA cards all at the same time. At least I saved on my credit card bill for a week.

Want one more reason why I like Saratoga? The neighborhood. On the way home from the cleaners I passed trainer Neil Howard running. So I stopped to take a picture of him. He stopped to chat, any excuse to stop running.

We stood on the corner and talked about Succeed and his stakes-winning horse Parade Ground, both retired from strained suspensories. Howard makes me feel better anyway. He said you could have blown him over with a feather when he heard that Parade Ground's career was over. I told him about a horse I galloped for Mark Hennig down in Florida. He said, "That big Affirmed colt." Horse trainers are sharp, that's for sure. So we stood there talking about horses getting hurt. If you ever deal with horses and something goes wrong, just go talk to someone else who deals with horses. You will at least understand that you are not alone. And trust me, that helps. What also comes to mind as I write about living with horses is that they are simply the chosen context in my life. You can interchange my horse experience all the way through this book with your chosen passion and come out with the same moral.

Eventually I let Howard get back to his run and I went home with a little more perspective on Succeed's injury. I can't help but think about Real Quiet, Victory Gallop, Charismatic and all the other horses injured day after day. Isn't that something—I just slipped

Victory Gallop in there. The Whitney hero retired with a leg injury. Just par for the agonizing course.

I can feel myself freeze as I read the headlines in the *Form* each morning. Every person in racing has a Succeed. Saratoga is the greatest racing town in the world but the Thoroughbred takes the heat. The Triple Crown, the Breeders' Cup, Del Mar or Saratoga—the horse gets stretched to the limit for events to take place. As Howard just told me, it's the good ones who get hurt.

Today is Alabama Day. Silverbulletday is 1-2, which means you can put up two to make one, for the $400,000 stakes. And in racing, we better appreciate her today because she might be gone tomorrow.

On the up side, I started my new job today. Rode my first trotter. Sorry, drove my first trotter today. Fun time, nothing to it. I drive

Sharing time—and life—with horses. *(Deirdre Davie)*

Appogee on Tuesday night in a celebrity (or joker) event at the raceway. I met my trainer, Paul Zabielski, today. He rode along on the cart and gave me some pointers.

I told him I wasn't worried. "At worst I bail out, right?" He about yanked me out of the seat and told me (six times), "Whatever you do, don't bail out." He also told me I was the perfect size—that's a first. I'm supposed to go back on Monday for some speed work. As they say on the trotting side, some modocking.

On my way out of the harness side of Saratoga, I stopped by the swimming pool. I was told through e-mail about a horse named Band Leader who swims laps every day. Sure enough, Band Leader was in the middle of his 40-minute swim. The 7-year-old trotter grunted his way around. He actually stops swimming and wades throughout the exercise. He'll just stop and groan, like he's rebelling or resting, and then resume again.

The horse holds a world record and a track record at Saratoga, which I was told don't count because he's a gelding. Sounds like a bad deal for Band Leader to me. Horses are the most generous creatures we know. Band Leader swam around his pool and I swear he looked at me, right in the eye and begged me to let him out of the pool. He acted like he enjoys swimming but also like he would like to get out anytime. He's supposed to qualify on Tuesday night and run back on Saturday.

ALABAMA MAMA
Sunday, August 22

Roberto Luna flipped the reins over the filly's head and strolled out of the winner's circle. No halter, no shank, Silverbulletday just walked home, up the long Saratoga stretch. She was barely blowing. Her sides moving like an afternoon nap. She looked toward the infield and back to the grandstand when a rain-soaked mother yelled, "Horse of the Year!"

Silverbulletday, Luna, hotwalker Claudia Esquivel and assistant/ exercise rider Peter Hutton trekked through the Saratoga sand away from the Alabama Stakes and toward the test barn. Silverbulletday could have done the day herself. The champion filly just meandered to the barn, no stress in her legs, no weariness in her eyes. She could have won the ninth, tenth and today's Ballerina Stakes.

It was epic Saratoga. A slow, menacing misty rain. Dark clouds in every direction. A 40-cents-on-the-dollar favorite. Fans peeking off every ledge, every nook and cranny of the ancient masterpiece.

I knew Silverbulletday would win. That was squarely in my brain; but I kept thinking of Secretariat, Man o' War, and the Saratoga demons that caused their upsets. That's why people stood four deep on the outside rail, in the rain—to see for themselves.

The horses broke with a cheer from the crowd, and when announcer Tom Durkin bellowed, "Silverbulletday has taken the lead," the place went wild. Forget the demons, this filly is that good.

Jerry Bailey made three moves during the 1¼-mile race. He took her back. He let her go. And he pumped his fist. That's about all there was to do. Bailey changed his cross once at the head of the stretch—OK maybe four moves. Then gave her a slow-motion hand-ride from there. She won by nine in a waltz.

Silverbulletday could have found the test barn without Luna. The finish line without Bailey. The greatness without any of us. She's in her own world without any distractions.

"She's in a league of her own. There's just something about her. I don't know what makes them good. She's not anything spectacular to look at but she is one amazing filly," Hutton said. "She's not even blowing and she'll eat a full feed tub tonight."

And why not? She had just gone for a stroll. A stroll for her, a struggle for the rest. Silverbulletday annihilated her rivals, collecting $240,000 and running her lifetime record to 13-for-15. Saratoga has another hero.

Back at the test barn, Luna slipped the bridle off in the shedrow—no stall needed, just a routine switch. The filly gulped water out of the bucket while Luna filled it up with the high-pressure hose. She walked around the shedrow, drank her water, got a bath, gave a urine sample and went home. As she neared her barn she dove toward the grass and tried to roll. She is still, after all, a horse.

Silverbulletday stretches the Alabama. *(Harlan Marks)*

Luna would not allow either, which disappointed me. Here's a horse in a man's world trying to salvage one horse moment. No grass and no roll. She's too much horse to allow the simple pleasures.

Sure enough, when Luna hung her hay net, she dove at it like the whole Alabama thing was no more than going without hay for half the day.

Hutton summed it up: "I'll never be near another horse like this. It's an honor to be around her, let alone ride her."

Maybe that is what Saratoga is about. An honor. I feel honored to be able to walk next to Silverbulletday after the Alabama. To stand and watch such brilliance. To pet her. To try to tell you about it. I took another walk after this one. I left trainer Bob Baffert's barn on the backside of the main track and started toward the grandstand and my bike. I slummed it today, jeans, sneakers, baseball hat. Hey, it was raining. This is my favorite walk in Saratoga. It's the first time I'm alone after watching a once-in-a-lifetime performance. Being able to walk home with Luna and Silverbulletday, watching her slip the shank from her lip for fun, seeing her dive into her hay, listening to stablemate Miss Wineshine nicker at her when she returned. That's what I'll remember.

This walk was reflective, but not as peaceful. Must have been earlier than the last time I walked this walk. As you might have guessed, I don't wear a watch.

Cars were lined up from the grandstand to Nelson Avenue. I walked and looked inside the traffic.

Seven cars in a row were on cell phones. A man smoking a cigar next to his lady checking her makeup in the mirror of a Cadillac. Two laid out in the backseat of a Lincoln. Five people in a Volvo from New Jersey. A Cadillac cut off a Maxima. A Maxima gave the universal signal. A man asked me if I'm working on the journal. Six people in a Cadillac asked me if I won today. One old guy in a beat up Grand Am. Four in a Mercedes. Two men in a Porsche Carrera from New Jersey. Another Porsche from New Jersey with a "Kahuna" license plate. The Ameripride Linen and Apparel Service van just looked for a hole in the traffic.

Silverbulletday's owner Mike Pegram tried to duck the crowd and got stopped by a man who said, "Mike, you know me from . . . hey Joey, where's he know me?" Pegram tried to be polite. Joey came over and explained where they know each other from. Pegram gave another universal signal (not the finger one): "Yeah, that's right. How you doing? OK. Great. Good to see you." And he split. Bob Baffert hopped into the driver's seat of a baby blue Windstar minivan with Mike and grandson Gator Pegram in the back. License plate W50-2YK. They got right in line behind the linen van.

I found my mountain bike and went across traffic, back into the grandstand. On my way out of the other side, I saw Bailey and his family. It was getting dark and Bailey was still faced with autograph seekers and questions. A man asked the jockey if she's the best one ever. Bailey just smiled. "One of them."

Silverbulletday was the best today. That's what counts.

HEART RACING
Monday, August 23

Horse racing. It's more addicting than potato chips, coffee, heroin, naps. If you ever won a photo, lost a photo, patched up a horse, bet out, got shut out, galloped a horse, hurt a horse, fell off a horse, won a triple, if you ever were Mike Smith, Pat Johnson, Lizzie Hendriks, Susan Bunning, Shug McGaughey, Furlough, Bourbon Belle, Proud Run. Or if you ever talked to them, knew them, saw what they go through, then horse racing is in your blood. It is your blood.

Once you get in, you can't get out. It won't be easy, it won't be timid, it won't be quiet. Horse racing will rock your world.

Sunday at Saratoga rocked those eight players and everyone around them.

Check the program, the overnight, the *Form* and you won't see Hendriks or Proud Run anywhere under Saratoga. But they were Saratoga on Sunday. Proud Run won the New Castle Handicap at Delaware Park. And if you were anywhere near the Saratoga racing office you knew it. Hendriks gallops, breezes, makes most of the decisions for Proud Run. She was in the office at 3:39 p.m. for the seventh at Delaware (if you play with the TV channels, you can watch other racetracks in the office). Hendriks' mother, Katharine Merryman owns Proud Run. Hendriks and her husband, Ricky, train Proud Run. The 5-year-old mare is Lizzie's pride—when you are involved like this, a horse represents you. That horse is your brain. Your soul. Everything you have goes into that horse. Not that the rest of the world doesn't matter, but this is your work, your love. What happens to her on the racetrack is what defines your life.

I work for them, that's why I know this story. Proud Run trains over the Oklahoma track at Saratoga every day. She is one of the faceless/nameless creatures that circles the oval each morning. She's nameless, faceless to you, but she's the Hendriks' stable everything. The New Castle sent her earnings up over $400,000 and paid for the family's trip to Saratoga this year. Like last year and maybe even the year before that.

I took two photos of Lizzie watching the television. In one, she's stone still as Proud Run nears the far turn. In the second she's euphoric as Proud Run hits the wire. The two photos—that is horse racing. One watching and one celebrating. That's what we live for. Those minutes of spectating when you hope and pray and those moments of pure exhilaration when everything comes together. We went nuts in the secretary's office. Proud Run won by a head. It hit Lizzie the most. It hit me because I know the story behind it, because I gallop the horse a couple of times a week. It hit trainers Lisa Lewis and Tom Voss and the guy who was rooting for third-place finisher Absolutely Queenie, too. We all know the magnitude of winning a race, the latitude of what went into it. That's why it is addicting. Horse racing might have lost some of its characters and camaraderie, but for a competitive sport, the spirit still lives.

For everyone.

Bourbon Belle and Pat Johnson wishing for the line. *(Harlan Marks)*

Furlough and Mike Smith exhale. *(Barbara D. Livingston)*

About an hour later jockey Mike Smith and trainer Shug Mc-Gaughey won the Grade I Ballerina in the last desperate stride with Furlough. Pat Johnson and Susan Bunning lost the Ballerina in that same stride aboard Bourbon Belle. Furlough is the foundation of horse racing. A blue-blooded Kentucky bred, made for Saratoga stakes. Bourbon Belle is the mortar of horse racing. The fluid in between the joint. They converged in the last foot of the seven-furlong Ballerina. Mike Smith going for his first Grade I victory of the meet and Pat Johnson going for his first Grade I ever. Horse racing at its polar best. Bourbon Belle on the lead and hanging on, Furlough in the back and charging.

The fans knew it was coming. And they froze. They roared without knowing they were roaring. When the wire came, their lives were in their throats. They stood there, dumbfounded, awestruck. "Who got it?" fills the air. Like somehow somebody else should know. Like everyone didn't just see the same thing. Then come the predictions. "Three. Six. The outside. Inside by a head. Smith. The shipper. The black." Then back to "Damned if I know. Too close for me. Can't tell by the angle. Look at the slow mo. Yeeehhhh."

Then back to silence. They waited for the photo. Most have losing tickets in their pockets but this race was so good, they just had to know who won. Finally, the six flashed above the three. Furlough and her royal Ogden Phipps foundation nosed out the family project, Bourbon Belle.

Think I'm addicted?

I've spent lifetimes in the sauna with Mike Smith, watching him pump iron and lose pounds. I have a standing invitation to vacation in New Mexico with him. I was with his wife Patrice when he broke his back last year. I saw him in the hospital a couple days later, trying to stick a coat hanger down his cast to stop the itch. I know Mike Smith. He is a friend. He had all the business before he was hurt and now he struggles to find that business again. Mike Smith is the eighth-leading jockey this year at Saratoga. Last year, he was in front and riding horses like Jersey Girl and Coronado's Quest. All that was in my heart when I saw the famous black and cherry silks of Furlough. Shug and Mike are a team. Now here they come for their first big score at Saratoga this year. But who's in the way?

The game Bourbon Belle and my new friend Pat Johnson. Remember our conversation earlier in the meet, when he stood Bourbon Belle in for me—and himself—after winning the Honorable Miss? Now I root for him. And Susan Bunning, who said her last win was for all the little people. The little horse had flown through a quarter in 22 seconds and a half in 44⅘. Three quarters in 1:09⅗. One more furlong. Mike Smith and Furlough in my left eye, Pat Johnson and Bourbon Belle in my right. Either one. Neither one.

Furlough caught Bourbon Belle. It took her every inch of the race, but she caught her. Pat Johnson was stoic in defeat, even faked an upbeat interview for espn2. Susan Bunning was crying. She hugged Johnson, patted Bourbon Belle. I wanted that inch back, just to see her exult in the moment. But she didn't crumble. That's the addicting part, coming that close. It's being in the moment. Letting the moment do what it wants to you. That is horse racing.

Mike and Shug are addicted, too. They live and die with horses like Furlough, a come-from-behind sprinter who needs more to go her way than a baby turtle. She broke through the gate in the same

Proud Run and Lizzie Hendriks gallop on the Oklahoma. *(Richard Hendriks)*

race last year. She was 1-for-11 leading up to this Ballerina. Smith popped up on the scale after the race like a man just out on good behavior. He pumped his fist. He smiled. Shug was just plain relieved. Smiling, too. Smith and Shug needed a moment. Just like Hendriks and Proud Run. Like Bourbon Belle, Johnson and Bunning.

Me? I'm just happy to be near the moments.

SARATOGA SUNRISE

Tuesday, August 24

Today was one of those mornings when I wave to the guard at the stable gate and marvel at what awaits. It's the promise of potential. The brilliance of nature. The sun's coming up, shining through the mist. Horses and riders are heading out for the first set of the day.

I am now in a painting, a Barbara Livingston photo, a dream. Stop and look around. Get out of the car and take a picture. Then get on a horse and gallop through the mist. My horse cuts the fog with his rattling air. Eyelashes bead with the morning. Faces are cleansed. Life seems easier. At least for a moment.

Saratoga in the fog.

The sun comes up—like nowhere else—at Saratoga. *(Barbara D. Livingston)*

Horses always go better in the fog. They relax. Maybe they're taking in the moment, like the humans. The fog slows them down, holds them in motion. Horses have more grace, more rhythm, in the fog—especially Saratoga fog.

Saratoga fog is it's own weather element. Like rain forest rain. Or Colorado snow.

Take a deep breath. Paradise. Only in Saratoga can a morning feel like this.

I haven't eaten, barely slept, but the air keeps my sanity. Stifles my anxiety. Cushions the blows.

The sun eventually comes through and the fog is gone. Now, can that feeling stay? That's the mystery. Can you keep that feeling of peace for the day?

FRIENDS AND FALLS
Wednesday, August 25

Need a shortcut to the local hospital? I know them all. Spent the afternoon in the Saratoga Hospital. Today was a disaster, horses fell everywhere. I survived steeplechasing at its worst, but my friend Chip Miller fell at the second fence down the back.

We were head and head, talking to each other—he wondered what I was doing coming up his inside this early in the race. I said I couldn't help it and told him to just sit still. Then we jumped. His horse, Cambridge Bay, disappeared. I could hear Chip in the corner of my ear yelling "Colvin" to the jockey on his outside. They had bumped right before the fence. So Chip went down. It looked like an easy fall. I could see his horse's head hitting the ground and I could see Chip slipping his reins and getting away from the impact. It looked like an easy fall, but you never know what's coming from behind. A fall in a horse race is like an accident on the highway. One car bounces off the median strip, spins out, taps another, and all hell breaks loose.

Cambridge Bay slid and tipped over. Solitary Shot, following behind, slammed broadside into him and fell right into Chip. The

Chip Miller and Cambridge Bay (left) before disaster. *(Barbara Livingston)*

horse landed square on my friend. There are two major ways to get seriously hurt while riding steeplechase races—falling square on your head or neck, and having a horse fall on you.

Colvin Ryan and Jericho Warning fell at the next fence, bringing down Splashdown and Toby Edwards. It was the ugliest race of the meet, one that makes me wonder what the hell I'm doing with my life.

I cantered home fourth, beaten a football field but at least still upright. Then my role changed.

I made it back to the jocks' room and started asking about my friend. Called first aid. Did anyone see Chip get up? All I saw when I pulled up was a slew of people peering on the other side of the hedge where Chip had fallen. And, unfortunately, the horrible replay on the TV when I got back to the room. Watch a 1,000-pound horse fall like a broken elevator right on top of your best friend and see how unnerved you get.

Finally, I found out he was on his way to Saratoga Hospital.

I showered like the hot water was out and made a run for it, through the racetrack gate and to my car.

Amazingly enough, I followed the ambulance to the hospital and continued the deductive reasoning process—the siren's not on, the lights aren't flashing and they're stopping at red lights. It can't be too bad. I recognized the bottom of Chip's boots through the back window. They moved once in a while, another good sign. This is the only sport where you say "yeah he's OK, he's moving."

I met Chip and Colvin as they were carried out of the ambulance, both taped down to their backboards. They were talking, or more like groaning. Both let down a little when they saw me—you could see them relax at the sight of a friend.

They put my friends next to each other in the corner room, the same one we were in last year when another friend, Keith O'Brien, had a fall. I've been in this hospital as patient and visitor too many times and begin to feel like an old war veteran, squirming at the white walls and stale hospital smell.

We talked a little about the race, or what they remembered. Chip and Colvin complained of backaches. Both tried, to no avail, to find some level of comfort strapped to a board. They asked for something to drink. They were in the sauna two hours before, and were desperate for something to help the pasty state of their mouths. Like all hospitals, this one wouldn't let them drink anything. How can the most natural substance known to man, water, hurt anyone? I dodged the nurses and went for water. Poured it into their mouths from a Dixie cup. Like I gave them life. I snuck back for more water. They lapped it up.

Jump jockeys thrive on the independence, the pure feeling of speed and freedom. We are young at heart, that is for sure. My friends looked half the size and twice as old as they did a couple of hours ago. Their sweat-matted heads looked like baby doll heads on the white hospital sheets. There is no more helpless feeling than lying on a backboard, still dressed as a jockey, doctors prodding, assistants asking when your last tetanus shot was. Your flak jacket is cutting you in half, rubber bands around your wrists look so pathetic now. You are no longer a jump jockey, you are a broken boy looking for someone to carry you back to this morning, when you were free.

Chip and Colvin were wheeled to X-ray. Again, like all hospitals, wheeled to X-ray not into X-ray. We wait. I can't eat, can't sit, can't think. Just bouncing around the corridor thinking about Pinkie Swear tomorrow and my *Backstretch* deadline today.

Chip seemed to get better with time, Colvin went the other way—more uncomfortable, more uneasy with every minute. Chip, I could see in his face, was slowly ruminating his next move. I've been in his spot before, you start to wish you heeded the old jump jock creed—don't ever let them put you in the ambulance.

Chip and I have been best friends for 21 years, we communicate without a word being spoken. I can see the machinations forming in his battered head.

Eventually, Chip made it into X-ray, I ran off to buy a pack of Tic-Tacs (the 1½ calorie breath mint) and a *People* magazine. I called my editor and explained that I'm still doing research for today's column. Don't force a column from a jockey. They waited. So did I. Finally, they wheeled Chip out of the radiation chamber and back to his corner room. I was shocked at the sight of Colvin: he is the oldest jump jock in the room and he looked 100 years older by the minute. Chip looked ready for a pizza, except when he moved. Then he looked ready for a masseuse and a whirlpool.

We sat, stood, shuffled around the room waiting to hear if the mentally broken were physically broken as well.

Chip was not. Colvin was iffy. Chip came home with me and Colvin went to Albany Medical Center for an MRI. I think he'll be OK—my diagnosis is exertion combined with trauma combined with exhaustion. Of course I'm no doctor.

Chip's on my couch now. Two prescriptions filled, a Pepper's Market turkey sandwich in him, a large coffee and peanut butter from Ben and Jerry's. He's meant to ride his best horse, Popular Gigalo, in the meet's most important steeplechase tomorrow. He swears he can do it. He can barely walk but he's still a jump jockey and he will ride tomorrow.

I just passed my buddy on the way upstairs with a cup of tea in my hand, said I had to go write about him; he told me to wait until tomorrow.

SWEATING

Thursday, August 26

From *A Farewell to Arms,* by Ernest Hemingway.

"'They ought to feed them better. We are big eaters. I am sure there is plenty of food. It is very bad for the soldiers to be short of food. Have you ever noticed the difference it makes in the way you think?'"

"'Yes,' I said. 'It can't win a war but it can lose one.'"

I'm on my way to the sauna. Don't bother me. Don't talk to me. Don't cross me. Food is an amazing thing. I think all wars, divorces, disasters could have been avoided with food. The next time you're about to go off on something, stop and eat and see what happens—I swear you won't even remember what the problem was.

I will try not to lose the war. Hemingway put it right. At this point, I'm not trying to win anything, I'm just trying to survive. Trying not to lose. Winning the New York Turf Writers Cup is on the other side of an indomitable wall, with which I stand face to face.

So I head now to the track to lose four, five, six pounds. It's bad. I ride Pinkie Swear in the Turf Writers, the richest jump race at Saratoga. We'll see what happens.

The Turf Writers is a $100,000 stakes, and before you start counting my money, I make 10 percent of what my horse makes. If by the grace of God Pinkie Swear wins, I make $6,000. Not much for the biggest race of the Saratoga meet but enough to write a killer column. And enough to do all I can to make the weight.

Writing a journal like this makes me realize how integral success in my life is to this project. When Succeed ran well at the beginning of the meet and Pinkie won a couple of weeks ago, my writing followed suit. When life is good, writing an energetic, inspired column is easy.

But of course, nothing good has happened yet today.

It's a dreary day at the track, looks like the greatest drought of this century will soon be over. The rain is coming. I don't know what Pinkie will think of the soft turf; for his sake, my sake and (follow me) the journal's sake, let's hope he can roto-till right through it. Just another question as I trudge toward the abyss.

I've been dieting for 10 days and can't get near 140. That's where the sauna comes in, I will spend my afternoon there. Want to join me? This is Hokan revisited, at least the being fat part.

The sauna, sweat box, hot box, cooker, is where I will spend the afternoon today. It's made up of three rooms: one dry sauna, one warm room and a steam room. So take your pick, look down the barrel. Shower first, take two towels, cover yourself with baby oil, sit in the steam room (the hottest section) until you can't stand it, come out into the warm room. Sit and sweat. That's about the extent of it. Wait as long as you can before you grab the hose (a cold water hose runs constantly). It will become your lifeline. But don't drink

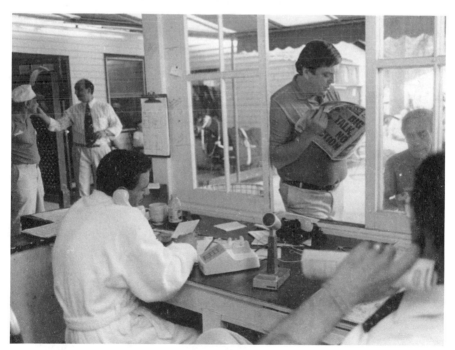

Welcome to the jocks' room. *(Deirdre Davie)*

the water, only run it over your head and into your mouth. Whatever you do, don't drink the water. Swallow a mouthful of water and extend your time in hell. You can try to read, but I can't get through a paragraph in the sauna. Some people can. I can't comprehend a word. Imagine being under the foil of a Jiffy Pop. So just sit and try not to pop.

The first two pounds aren't bad. You can handle that. You're hot but it's still tolerable. Aaron Gryder, Mike Smith, Jose Santos, Joe Deegan keep you company. Let them do the talking; it's easier to listen than talk in here.

Everyone always seems like they're handling it better than me. It's the one place in the world where I don't have something to say. You can slap me around, curse my mother, rip my book in here. I have no fight, just let me be. This is my time to stew.

When you need a break, go out and check your weight but count on being disappointed. Every jockey gets on the scale the same way. Slip off the towel, your shower shoes and keep one hand on the screw to the right of the scale. Don't take your finger off until you're balanced, then gently release your finger and hover. Look at the numbers for at least a full minute, one of these days they will drop. One of these days, if you stand still long enough on the scale, your weight will just drop off. Eddie Arcaro, Steve Cauthen, Braulio Baeza have stood on top this same scale in this same paralyzed state of mind.

After you check your weight and know that it is that bad, go back into the sauna. Your stool, your new towel, your frustration. Don't overheat, make sure you keep sweating.

If you have to, come out and take a cold shower and start the whole process again. Avoid getting goose bumps, if your skin bumps, forget it, you're done. Eventually you'll get within a pound of what you want, then the boiling point intensifies; the last pound is harder than the first four. It will take you hours to lose that last pound. Go ahead and shave, you held out this long, it will take your mind off it. Be slow, prolong the time when you actually have something to do. This is the one time you wish you had more face to shave. You go up, down, sideways, ears, chin, under your nose, down your neck, your sideburns, around again. Shaving never meant so much. You fight the urge to start shaving your chest.

Check your weight again.

Still a half to go. Get the soap and lather up, again and again. The movement and the soap will take that last half, well quarter, you never get to where you want. When you absolutely can't go in there again, it's time to get out. You're never finished in the sauna, you just stop. You'll be OK, take an ice-cold shower, take a nap, guzzle bee pollen and ginseng. Ignore the "You look like hell" comments from Shane, Mario, Simon and the rest of the room. Hop up and down, growl and get dressed. You are now able to do the weight and ride the race. Face the war.

So do you want to join me? It will all be over in six hours. I'll be at Sperry's eating a five-course meal by 8 p.m. That seems a long way away right now. See you in five pounds. When the war is over.

THE GREATEST RIDE
Friday, August 27

Yesterday I talked about food. Today it's water. Just the essentials now. Tomorrow will be fire (the Travers) and Sunday will focus on shelter. That's a stretch, but I do have to talk about rain. Saratoga stinks in the rain. It poured half the morning. Nothing like galloping horses in a monsoon. I spent the rest of the morning slogging around in a pair of drenched Levi's. I did manage to get to the Country Cafe for a "making-up-for-lost-time breakfast." Two peach pancakes, one apple cinnamon pancake, two scrambled eggs, a side of toast, one sausage patty, two coffees and a large orange juice. Was I the one complaining about my weight yesterday? That wasn't me. I feel great today. I can't reach the keyboard due to my new flapjack belly but, all the same, everything's perfect. Food, the greatest show on Earth.

So why water today? Rain changes everything at Saratoga. The turf races (my favorite part of any card) switch to the sloppy main track, horses run out of form and walking around town is a real drag. Rain on the parade.

So here I am fighting the urge to nap. I will get over to see Banshee Breeze run in the Personal Ensign later today. If I trained Banshee Breeze, she wouldn't step foot on this track. Sloppy tracks are simply muddy water on top of a rock-hard base. But that's why I'm the writer and Carl Nafzger is the trainer. Like Chuck Simon said, being the trainer is the difference between making suggestions and making decisions. Scratching Banshee Breeze is simply a suggestion.

Yesterday, I lost my weight and the race. Pinkie Swear ran OK, finished fifth, floundered in the soft going. Campanile, a horse I used to ride, led the whole way to win his second stakes of the meet. My man Chip finished behind me, so I guess I'm not writing about him either.

I wish one of us could have pulled it off yesterday. Chip went home, more sore than he was right after the fall—that's what losing will do to you.

The greatest.
(Doug Lees)

He said to me in the jocks' room before the race, "You know, everybody keeps telling me not to do it, what am I trying to prove? They just don't get it. It's not to prove anything and doesn't have anything to do with being heroic. It's just to ride a good horse. That's all."

Jockeys are in it to ride good horses. To miss a ride on a good horse at Saratoga—you better be more than sore.

Good horses, that's what Saratoga exists upon and what we all thrive upon. All I could think of as I watched Chip limp around the room yesterday was my hero Joe Aitcheson. All he wanted to do was ride a good horse. He made it his life. Joe stands atop the sport of American steeplechasing by placing a number that carries a DiMaggio 56, a Beamon 29, a Bannister 3:59, for the rest of us to merely dream about. Joe Aitcheson won 440 steeplechase races, a record that will never be broken (I've been at it for 12 years and have won about 135). The greatest victory along Joe's 440 quest was Happy Intellectual at Saratoga in 1977. I'll never forget being a 7-year-old child and hearing about how Joe had pulled off a Saratoga miracle.

I couldn't write a book without a Joe Aitcheson chapter. The greatest steeplechase jockey in history and my one true real-life hero. Joseph Leiter Aitcheson Jr. Simply Joe, in steeplechasing.

Everyone has a Joe Aitcheson story. Everyone has a Joe Aitcheson and Happy Intellectual story. Here's one I received from column reader Lillian Cushny:

> I'm writing to tell you a true occurrence that I was witness to and was reminded of when you wrote of Chip Miller.
>
> The story is almost identical if you back up 22 years, change the jockey's age to 20 years older and change the last line to, "and he'll ride next week on his best horse." When I was a teenager in 1977 I was galloping horses for Mike Freeman and that year in Saratoga Joe Aitcheson took a galloping job with him for the meet.
>
> During the third week, Joe fell in a race and he was hurt badly enough to not gallop in the morning or to

ride any races. He was 49 years old. He was, however, supposed to ride Mrs. Ogden Phipps' Happy Intellectual in
the Turf Writers Cup the closing week. So the day before
the Turf Writers we hear that Joe is going to come out
and ride the pony. A car pulls up to the gate of our yard
the way it does when it is going to deposit some important owner or jockey—ordinary visitors do not arrive this
way. The car has brought Joe and he's wearing a neck
brace.

People go out to greet him and say hey, "How's it
going," because he's normally very friendly and talkative.
But today he's not talking, I don't remember him saying
one word. He also can barely walk, that's why he was
dropped at the yard gate because that's where the pony is
tied up. I think at this point people tried to talk him out

Joe Aitcheson after one of his falls. *(Winants Brothers)*

of this idea but he started climbing up the mounting block and two of the guys got on either side of him to hold him steady. Then they had to pick him up and put him on the back of the pony. He sat astride but he never moved, never spoke, and I'm not sure how much he was breathing.

The pony was never untied and he never even walked in a circle much less went to the track. Then the two guys helped him get off and put him back in the car. At this point I'm thinking, I suppose it was worth a try but it appears that he cannot possibly ride tomorrow.

I'm sure you know how the story ends: he not only rides Happy Intellectual but he wins the New York Turf Writers Cup of 1977.

I saw a chart once of the silent movie stuntman cowboy Tom Mix, and it was a chart of all of the places in his body where he had taken bullets or had broken bones. I think that the same kind of chart could be made of Joe Aitcheson's body. He used to ride with football shoulder pads, predating safety vests, because as legend tells it he had broken his collarbones so many times that they had simply been removed.

Nothing about Joe Aitcheson is legend; he is the toughest, most dedicated man who ever lived. Steeplechasing just happened to be his passion. Riding Happy Intellectual in the biggest race of the season was simply the only way there was to do it.

Here's how Joe, who still gallops horses at Laurel Park, told the story:

"Happy Intellectual was a decent horse, but he hadn't been running that great. When he got tired in the stretch he would ease up and take care of himself. But he was the best stakes horse I had to ride at the time.

"Well, the week before the Turf Writers I had a fall on a horse named Sun Sign who just tried to run right through the hurdle. It was like he picked up one foot and then put it back down; that was the last thing I remember. I woke up and there were a lot of people around me. Knocked me silly for a little while. I said if you help me up and get me on my feet, I'll feel better. Then when I got about halfway up, my neck hurt so bad I told them to put me back down.

"So I went to the hospital; I remember the next day they let me get up and go to the bathroom and I looked in the mirror. It looked like a Japanese wrestler, straight from my ears on down; it was swelled up. The biggest, fattest neck I've ever seen. The doctor said they couldn't understand why my neck didn't break. They kept me in there for four days, they gave me a neck brace and some medication to take.

"I wanted to keep galloping some horses. I tried to ride an old horse for Mike Freeman, I couldn't do it. I was totally out of control. I got off that horse and just said I'm going to go on home.

"But Mikey Smithwick couldn't find a decent rider for Happy Intellectual. I thought if I could get a track vet to get me a prescription for some better pain pills I'd be all right. So I did, and they took care of me pretty good. I could walk, but I couldn't jog. I got on one old jumper and cantered around a little in that lot over at the jumping barn. The concussion of the horse's feet hurt so bad.

"I figured with the pain pills I'd be OK, but after laying around the hospital for that long, I was afraid I'd get real tired. One of the girls who worked for Mikey had a double seated bicycle; that was the best exercise I could get. I could just pedal along behind her without moving too much. That was the most exercise I did before the race.

"So the day of the race, the big problem was getting me on the horse. They used to saddle them outside under the trees, but Mikey took Happy up in the saddling stalls so no one could see us. He was a big strong man and picked me up, I think he had some help; they put me on real slow.

"Happy used to always run on the lead so he broke in front and everything was going good. The last three-quarters of a mile, my legs just got rubbery. I was exhausted. I had a grip of his mane and just was sitting on him, just hanging on.

"Coming to the last fence I said, 'oh man, please,' if he just pecks at it or something, I'm going to topple off. But he jumped it great. He's on the lead and I could hear the whips popping and I knew they were closing in. I went through the motions of hitting him. Like a feather, I'm sure. It didn't help him much.

"On the second horse was a jock from England and for some reason he was way on the outside. He was the one that was going to beat us. I couldn't turn my head but when Happy saw that horse out there, that old sucker just shifted gears and kicked in, me hanging on. I had a hold of the mane and was just going through the motions.

"He just took off; it was the biggest thrill I ever had in racing. I didn't expect him to win and, after all the turmoil, the fall, getting exhausted and me just hanging on—that old horse shifting gears and kicking in. . . . He held that other horse safe and won.

"If there was any way I could, I always rode. I used to take horse Butozolidan until they said it killed a few people; it would mess up your red blood cells. I always rode when I could. I rode with a cracked collarbone, but then you could just ride with the good hand.

"The neck, it was more painful. The Turf Writers was the big race of the meet. Saratoga is always very special. I rode well up until I got exhausted. I don't think I looked that bad. Some people thought I was crazy or silly, but no one tried to talk me out of it. If it wasn't the Turf Writers, I don't think I would have ridden.

"For some reason that horse dug in, maybe it had something to do with the way I felt. Horses are smart, so much smarter than most people think they are. I was resigned to getting beat but that old horse just did it all on his own; I was extra baggage.

"They had a little reception after the race, Mrs. Phipps and Mikey came down and got me. The doctor who let me ride was there, Dr. Esposito. I knew he would be all right when I heard his name, the same as Esposito's Bar right outside Belmont. I had to talk him into letting me ride, I told him I knew I could do it. He said to me when he let me ride, 'Don't make a fool out of me.'

"I think I had as much nerve as anybody. I thought I rode horses well, but I was never the smartest rider out there. My prerace butterflies were about being afraid of making a mental mistake. I knew I could do it physically but I was always afraid of making mental mistakes.

"Cordero was there when I came in the door after the race and told me, 'That was a great ride.' That was the first time a big-name jock ever made a comment like that to me. He knew that I had problems before the race. I forget the names of people I work with everyday, but I'll never forget Happy Intellectual in the Turf Writers.

"Getting into the Hall of Fame was the second biggest thrill to when that old horse took off on his own. . . . I guess I did it for the thrill of winning a race or whatever reason jump riders ride. I just loved to ride races."

MUSIC BOX
Saturday, August 28

Pinkie Swear was disappointing, but the longer you ride races, the better you get at handling disappointment. I can't complain. I've won one at the meet, and that was my goal. Two more chances and then Saratoga 1999 is over for the steeplechase jockey in me.

I ride Hudson Bay next week; he loves Saratoga as much as I do. He's 9 now and has won three races over the years here, with a track record, too. Of course, all those were with Arch Kingsley. Last year, Hudson forced me to my annual Saratoga nadir.

I had the call on him for the whole summer. I had watched some videotapes of his winning races. I schooled him for his race. And then I lost the A. P. Smithwick on Major Jamie. That cost me the ride on Hudson Bay. His trainer, Ricky Hendriks, told me this at the annual steeplechase cocktail party. Business is business and I don't blame Ricky. He basically followed owner's orders, doing what he had to do. So did I.

I cried.

I smiled and nodded to a few faces at the party, declined dinner at Sperry's and fell home. It was happening. The Saratoga curse had struck again.

Hudson was going to be even money in the race. I was having a huge year and felt like things were finally coming together. Then I lost the ride. Man, it was happening again. This was Hodges Bay getting beat at 3-2 in 1993. This was that saddle slipping to Roberto's Grace's tail and me falling off inches from the wire. This was my career; this was my life. Pure frustration, all a tease.

I couldn't believe I got taken off the horse before I even rode him. This had never happened before. Riding Hudson Bay at Saratoga is why you ride. This was the reward for sticking it out through 11 years of concussions and missed meals.

Now I was in my life again. Going home mad and going to the races next week as a spectator. I screened my calls all night. I read, watched some bad TV, vented in my journal and went to bed.

I didn't feel any better the next day. What would you do? I had been going to the Hendriks' barn every day and helping out after galloping for Leo O'Brien. I'd pick up a rake or clean a little tack. Now I didn't want to see that shedrow.

I went and galloped my horses at the O'Briens, spent all morning not answering "What the hell's wrong with you today?"

I finished my job there and made a decision. I went and raked the shedrow. I had a sore throat from all the "pride" I had to swallow. But I raked the shedrow.

Then I went to breakfast by myself and to the races by myself, where, of course, Hudson won by five. Still not answering my phone or talking to the world. That night I decided to go out.

I looked up the menu for Caffe Lena, a vintage folk music coffee house on Phila Street. I had been going past it for most of my Saratoga life, but never went in; too cautious. I had never heard of anyone going there. I had never heard of any of the singers who played there.

But that night, I knew was the night to go to Caffe Lena. Have you ever wanted to go out but were afraid that you would see someone and have to talk? That's how I spend most of my life and this night was the epitome of that. So I hopped on my bike and rode down

Nelson Avenue and made a left on Phila Street. I locked my bike and ran up the steps to Caffe Lena.

It was dark and quiet. An unassuming man at the top of the stairs who had never heard of Sean Clancy or Hudson Bay took my seven bucks. He showed me to my table and I sat down at MY table. I looked around and knew no one in the place. It felt good to be there. Like a hideout.

Then Pat Donahue walked past my table and stepped up on the small stage in the corner of the oldest coffeehouse in the world.

He said hello, tuned his guitar and played this:

> You've been knocked down. You've been dragged out.
> You've been misled and left for dead in a shadow of doubt.
> Over your shoulder is your only view and all I can say is
> don't let yesterday get the best of you
> 'cause this is this the beginning, this is not the end,
> this is not the time to be lying down and finally giving in.
> This world keeps spinning around and again
> and this is the beginning, this is not the end.
> Running leaves you breathless, standing makes you swoon.
> Fighting leaves you laying down and staying down
> and praying that it's all over soon
> but who knows what's waiting further on up the track.
> One thing I know is there ain't no road
> that's going to take you back
> 'cause this is the beginning, this is not the end.
> This is not the time to be lying down and finally giving in.
> This world keeps spinning around and again
> and this is the beginning, this is not the end.
> One day you're flying, next day you crawl,
> next day you don't know why but you can only go so high
> that you begin to fall.
> But sooner or later you go it alone
> and there's only one job and there's nobody's problems
> to solve but your own.
> 'Cause this is the beginning, this is not the end,

this is not the time to be lying down and finally giving in.
This world keeps spinning around and again,
this is the beginning this is not the end.
No, no this is not the end.

Hearing that one song was the most inspirational moment of my life. I can never remember an instant like that when I went from down to up that fast. I rode my bike home, with the CD *Life Stories* in clutch, alive and fired up.

Add music to food and the world would be at peace. Live music, especially a regular guy with an acoustic guitar singing to you, can ease all the stress from your head.

Pat Donahue became my favorite singer that no one ever heard of and Caffe Lena became my favorite place that no one knew existed.

I listened to the rest of the show but couldn't get "This Is the Beginning" out of my head. Did you ever wake up with a song in your head? This was the only time that I didn't want it out of my head. I sang it out loud on every set the next day.

I kept fighting, didn't give in, won the New York Turf Writers Cup a few weeks later and accomplished my one lifelong goal, becoming champion steeplechase jockey a few months later. Never did win one on Hudson Bay but that day was just the beginning.

Maybe I can win that Saratoga race on Hudson next week.

So that's something to look forward to anyway. My career at Saratoga Raceway is not.

My debut as a harness driver was a flop. I finished fourth—cough, cough—out of four. Appogee laughed at me. I think she knew I was an idiot; she barely got out of a trot. Old intelligent horses sense when you don't know what you're doing. I think she sensed it when it took me 10 minutes to get in the sulky. My trainer told me she needed a whip to motivate her but they wouldn't give us sticks (what were they thinking?).

Shaun Bridgmohan won the race in a photo over Shane Sellers, Joe Deegan passed me for third and I finished in the back by myself. Whenever you get beat, it feels like the whole world is watching. In actuality, it's the opposite, you're invisible without a witness in the world. But I was there. Like they say, it's not whether you win or lose, it's that you volunteered. I'm good at volunteering.

Today's volunteer is Banshee Breeze and tomorrow it's the meet highlight, the Travers. It's the premier weekend of the Saratoga meet. If you ever come to Saratoga, don't come on Travers weekend. The place gets Traversed. You can't move in the town this weekend. Every black-sock, sandal-wearing gawker (God love 'em) seems to have rushed off the beach and come to Saratoga for the weekend.

A few years ago, I called every restaurant from Albany to the Adirondacks looking for a table for two on Saturday night after the Travers. I gave up after this conversation with the hostess of some restaurant that I didn't like in the first place:

"Could I get a table for two on Saturday?"

"What are you, the Pope?"

So unless you're the Pope, stay away this weekend, watch the Travers at home on the couch and come on a weekend that you can walk down the street or eat without having to wear the rosary beads.

Beautiful Pleasure on her stage. *(Barbara D. Livingston)*

Drive and walk carefully. It's Travers Day. The roads are lined with cars, buses, horse-drawn carriages, campers—you name it, it's here. Cars park upside and backward on every corner in Saratoga. Fans packed Union Avenue beginning at daybreak. Nothing like the line at the gate on Travers Day.

I went to the press party last night. Besides defending steeplechasing to another press-boxed writer, the Travers was what we talked about. Look at the field and you'll understand why. Any horse in the race could win, from Menifee to Badger Gold. Everyone wants to know your pick. Everyone needs to know because no one knows. It's as wide open as a *Penthouse* forum.

Today is the defining moment. After the Travers, Saratoga is officially in remission.

Yesterday was anything but remission. Beautiful Pleasure got her revenge on Banshee Breeze in the Personal Ensign. Blame the mud, the weight, the lone speed, but the bottom line is Beautiful Pleasure smoked her. Alone on the lead, Beautiful Pleasure was never under serious pressure while winning the Grade I stakes by a little over two lengths. Banshee Breeze closed mildly to finish second, but it was all Beautiful Pleasure. I was thinking about writing a column based on her name and all the reasons it was just that yesterday. Decided against it, but I'll say this: it was a beautiful pleasure to watch a great filly beat another great filly in a race named for one more great filly.

After the race, the runner-up's trainer, Carl Nafzger, blamed the weight (she gave the winner 11 pounds) and the mud (the track was listed as sloppy). He also congratulated Beautiful Pleasure's trainer, John Ward, on a job well done. Complimented the winner a dozen times in a two-minute conversation. And why not. She is an amazing specimen.

Remember Silverbulletday, how petite and quiet she was—Beautiful Pleasure looks and acts like her evil big sister. She is like a colt. Big and strong, on her own mission. She carries a big belly and likes to show the world she's a tomboy. She tries to kick the groom when she gets a bath, she pulls the person on the shank around like a kite. She's just plain tough. She dwarfs Banshee Breeze. The two of them and third-place Keeper Hill walked around one after another. Banshee Breeze and Keeper Hill could be twins and then there is Beautiful Pleasure. The other two were covered in mud, up their noses, in their eyes, in their throats. They coughed like kids in an elementary school nurse's office. Beautiful Pleasure, with splashes of mud under her belly and hind legs, towered over them and walked like she was Miss Saratoga.

I took my walk from the test barn back to her barn in Horse Haven. I was on my bike, coasting behind her, just watching and keeping my distance. I cruised up next to her after we crossed Union Avenue; she whipped her head around and just scoffed at the audacity of a fool on a bike getting that close to a Saratoga stakes winner. But for the man on the shank, she would have come across the parking lot, pushed me over and kicked my bike. Maybe even spit on me. Remember the bully in school who would walk over and give you a finger in the chest? Beautiful Pleasure is his big, bad sister.

When she crossed Union Avenue, which is like crossing Times Square, she arched her neck and looked like Springsteen walking off the stage. The Personal Ensign had been over for an hour and Beautiful Pleasure showed her disdain for the traffic, which was there for her in the first place. She pranced down the horse path with a proud strut. If you didn't know she was a filly, you would swear this was the horse that just won the Travers. She looks like those old-time statues of horses, out of proportion. Muscled and stout. She looks more perfect than proportionless, but you just don't see many fillies who carry such a soldieresque presence.

Ward pulled a branch from a low-hanging oak as she was getting wound up. She took it in a snatch. Like she was a little ashamed at having to be fed but she was so damn hungry, too. Horses do this when they're proud of themselves. They grab the grass, or carrot, or hay in one quick lunge. Then they stand back and enjoy it, but with a nobleness no other species could possess.

Add Beautiful Pleasure to the list of Saratoga heroes this year. Victory Gallop, Behrens, More Than Ready, Pinkie Swear (hee hee), Honor Glide, Banshee Breeze, Silverbulletday, and Beautiful Pleasure, the iron maiden.

LEMONS AND JUNIORS
Sunday, August 29

"Come on Lemon Drop, lower the boom," thundered from the droves of Travers fans outside the paddock as the riders-up call was announced. Lemon Drop Kid balked and skidded toward the grass inside the walking ring of the Saratoga paddock. Jockey Jose Santos asked the crowd to chill with a smooth, conductor-like hand movement.

Santos used that same motion to conduct the ultimate Travers.

"If you could have the dream-perfect trip," Santos said after the $1-million victory, "this was it."

Santos placed Lemon Drop Kid into that dream, settled him right where he wanted. It was one of those races where you could see the winner from the start. Nothing went wrong, all the motions were river smooth. As they turned down the backside, Lemon Drop was ready to lower the boom while his seven rivals were all taking turns with nightmares.

Cat Thief was under pressure on the lead. Vision And Verse was lapped on Cat Thief and doing a little more than the rest. Badger Gold was pulling John Velazquez into the back of Cat Thief. Ecton Park was unsettled and stuck between horses. Menifee was rank early and behind a wall of horses. Unbridled Jet was way wide. Best Of Luck was barely on the grounds.

And there was Belmont Stakes winner Lemon Drop Kid, just cruising three wide and third. He was the catbird behind the steering wheel, waiting to turn the switch. He was comfortable right between the front-runners and the closers. Santos was perched up his neck with a long light hold, just waiting to finish the dream.

The jockey said he knew he was going to win the race at the half-mile pole.

It was an exciting Travers, but nothing like the Whitney or last year's Travers when Coronado's Quest battled Victory Gallop and Raffie's Majesty. Why? They were in doubt. This one never was.

Lemon Drop Kid (center) rounds the first turn. *(Harlan Marks)*

The finish of the dream-perfect trip. *(Barbara D. Livingston)*

Lemon Drop Kid canters back after the Travers. *(Harlan Marks)*

The final margin was close—he won by three-quarters of a length over Vision And Verse with Menifee third.

Santos made one mistake. He used too much stick, damn near threw it away. As Lemon Drop Kid walked into the winner's circle, the jockey lofted his whip to his valet in a celebratory toss. Went right over Dave's hand and into the crowd. And in another only-in-Saratoga moment, the fans gave it back.

That was Santos' only miscue all day.

His namesake knew it all along. Jose Santos Jr. is "only 5" but knows every person on the track and even knows who's going to win. He greets me with, "Sean Clance, you jump the fences. I'm going to jump the fences, it's not dangerous. My dad's scared of the fences, not me. I'm going to do both." He instantly holds your hand and starts walking, to the paddock, to the jocks' room, to the ice cream stand. You can't slow him down and you can't tell him otherwise.

Jose Santos Jr. practicing.
(Barbara D. Livingston)

"Lemon Dwop Kid," was his succinct answer to who was going to win the Travers. Smart kid. What a life. This kid will become a jockey; the racetrack is his playground. After the last race, when Dad was sitting on a stool with cameras, microphones and tape recorders occupying him, Little Joe (as he's sometimes called) was riding his own Travers. Adorned in a pair of yellow goggles and the errant Travers stick, Jose Santos Jr. replayed the Travers atop the jocks' room Equicizer—a practice horse.

The Travers tape was on the TV and Santos Jr. was Santos Sr.

"Whip him Little Joe."

"Not yet."

"Now Little Joe."

"Not yet."

When the horses turned for home on the TV, Little Joe got busy with a cross-the-body, right-hand stick and announced the race himself. He could be Tom Durkin and Jose Santos (Sr.) all at once.

"Come on Lemon," followed by a flourish of whip.

"Come on Lemon," followed by a celebration.

He even has the interview down.

"Did you know that horse was going to win?"

"I sat third, I took him outside and in the stretch I was in third. I whipped him when I broke out, I looked at the wire and knew I was going to win. And when we were passing the wire I just won the race. Bye."

ON THE BACK
Monday, August 30

On to wine. Enjoying a glass of Chardonnay as I write Monday's column. I was supposed to do 142 on Thursday and, admittedly, found myself a long way from it without any desire of getting there when I picked up the overnight to find Inca Colony in with 150. So I came home and celebrated with a glass of white and a jar of Green Mountain Gringo Salsa (and some chips). Look out.

It's the ninth inning. The vans start rolling in from faraway

Running Stag gallops
on the main track.
(Barbara D. Livingston)

lands—broken dreams and unfulfilled goals notwithstanding. Saratoga makes me sad this time of year. After the Travers, the air is gone; the life slowly fades. Now they ask you when you're leaving, not how long you're staying.

Breaks my heart. I stay to the bitter end. I don't leave a baseball game until the last pitch is thrown and I don't leave Saratoga until the last horse crosses the finish line. It's a long time between now and next year so why let go before you have to? It always feels like I would be letting the old girl down if I left without dancing the last dance.

And besides, I'm still writing this book.

I spent yesterday on the backside watching races. At least once a year I like to ride my bike over to the backside and see the sights, hear the sounds, smell the smells of this small sliver of racetrack life. It's a great place to watch a race.

The backside of Saratoga. *(Harlan Marks)*

Now my roommate comes up the stairs. "You still writing? Whew. On the wine, huh? Holy moly."

Thank you, Keith O'Brien, for the support.

Now where was I? On the backside. The backside is an intriguing place to watch the races. Stand by the rail as they run past. Then cross the ditch, the road and hover up to the TV to see what comes next. It's casual here. Relaxed and easy. No jackets, no ties, no fuss. Just a lot (for once I'm using the word correctly) of dirt, four betting windows, a slew of backstretch workers, some random fans, a couple of TVs, a geedunk stand (that's a term my father uses for quick food stores) and a view that you don't get from the front side. It's a cool spot to see the card. Characters everywhere. No airs. No egos. Just a collection of racing fans, betting, viewing, cheering and passing the afternoon. People are more real here, flopped against a tree, on the ground, on top of the white board fence. A sanctuary.

The stakes goes quietly past our world. Running Stag is cruising down the backside, about the same spot Lemon Drop Kid occupied the day before. Tom Durkin is but a faint sound in the background; the horses' beat resonates in your ear. That's the thing back here,

The sounds of silence. *(Harlan Marks)*

you hear sounds you wouldn't anywhere else. You can actually hear the horses' feet strike the ground. Occasionally, a jockey's yell. Running Stag looks like the winner even from here; Shane Sellers is motionless and soundless. And he does win the Saratoga Breeders' Cup. We watch it on the tube back here. It's like you're at the races but you're not at the races.

You can't half hear Durkin even on the TV so it's all a little hazy, but that adds to the atmosphere on the backside in the afternoon. When the favorite wins, the place barely makes a noise. When it's a longshot, the place is frantic trying to figure out who it is and how it's happening.

The backstretch is a positive. People never seem too tense on this side, morning or afternoon. Trainers will take the brunt of the stress but the rest of this world is full of quiet souls who are either hiding or living. It's lifetime college—you can put off the real world and build one of your own. It's up to you what kind.

It's a place for shots. Anybody can get a chance on the backside, whether it's training horses, rubbing horses or riding them. Stick around, you will make it here.

ROAD GRILL
Tuesday, August 31

Can I sleep now? My grill's busted. My VISA won't work. Hudson Bay isn't running. Even my street is closed for repairs. Times are tough around here. The Saratoga gods have a way to force you out, and today they're at their best. They want us gone.

I bummed breakfast at Beverly's, then went to Palmetto's Market for the *Form*. As I was in line to buy the $2.95 *Form*, I scrounged in my pockets to find two bucks, a MAC card and a VISA. So I stepped out of line and tried the ATM machine. Out of order. So I got back in line, at the end, and tried my VISA. It always works.

"It was denied. Sir, it was denied."

Huh?

"Sir, it was denied; what do you want to do?"

I want you to fix it, establish me a line of credit, come on help me out here. The guy behind the counter just looked at me impatiently. So off I went in search of a MAC machine. An hour later I resurfaced to claim my bag of groceries. I only wanted a *Form* but when I decided on the credit card, I figured I should shop. The total the first time was $13.90, this time it was $12.72. So I made money on the deal. Had to walk three miles but saved a buck eighteen. On my way home, I came across the "Detour" sign two houses down from mine, so around the block I went with the gods laughing (I could hear them) and finally arrived at home, three days later.

So that's the VISA and the road stories. Are you ready for the grill? Friends and fellow jump jockeys Toby Edwards and Cort Marzullo decided to have a Travers cookout. Great idea, but they only had one grill. You know what's coming next. They asked to borrow mine. I knew better. Lending your grill is right up there with being the only person in the family with a pick-up truck.

As my buddies put it: "In a funny turn of events, there we were driving, real slow down Lake Avenue and, you won't believe this part (laugh, chuckle, hoot), the wind got under the grill and it rolled to the back of the truck against the tailgate and (howl, guffaw, whoop)

Cort Marzullo has an "after-grill" smoke while I contemplate security deposits. *(Deirdre Davie)*

the tailgate just opened. You should have seen it, that grill bounced all over Saratoga."

Now what about my grill? I have a security deposit that was supposed to get me home. I think I killed the plants on the porch, broke one glass vase and now I'm missing a gas grill. I need toll money dammit.

"Oh, it still works; it's just dented a little. We were only going 45. We'll buy a new one if you want."

I haven't seen the old grill, the new grill, the money or the bill, so just put new grill on the list of things to do before the meet is up.

I took care of one item last night. Rode my bike into town after finishing Monday's column. I stopped by the Parting Glass, looked in the windows. Saw air and space. You know it's over when you can see through the Glass. A couple of die-hards drinking and throwing darts, some waiters making busy, an empty stage and untapped kegs. I looked for someone interesting and decided to ride around some more.

I went uptown to Broadway, same thing, rode my bike right down the sidewalk without having to slow down or yield once. I crossed the street and heard a race call. Pedaled over to the plate glass window in front of The Crafter's Gallery, where the Travers video was playing on a TV set. I sat on my bike, one foot on the railing, and watched the Travers in all its glory. The footage of Ridan and Jaipur, Buckpasser, Affirmed and Alydar, Chief's Crown, Forty Niner and Seeking The Gold was cool to see, especially on the barren streets of Saratoga. How about Affirmed and Alydar? That was some bump and some bummer. I couldn't imagine waiting for that showdown and seeing it end like that. Glad I was 8 and didn't know any better when it happened.

I left the movie theater and pedaled back to the Glass for one. Dull company and bitter drink, so I left and hit Ben and Jerry's. Rode my bike right in the store, another clue that the meet is winding down. It's not too bad really, almost nice to be able to get around, but still a little sad. I rode home with my large vanilla shake.

Can anybody do the theme to *M*A*S*H*? If you could hum it right here that would make the perfect transition. I turned on the TV while I finished my milkshake and found the last 10 minutes of the last *M*A*S*H* episode. Remember when Colonel Potter swings onto to his horse Sophie, looks down at BJ and Hawkeye, says farewell and rides off down the road and out of sight? Then BJ gives Hawkeye a motorcycle ride up to the chopper pad. They stand there and say their good-byes. Hawkeye climbs in the helicopter and BJ says he left him a note. When the chopper takes off Hawkeye looks down and sees "GOODBYE" spelled out in rocks. Then the theme song comes on for the last time and BJ rides his motorcycle off the chopper pad.

And I went to bed.

THE SOUNDS

Wednesday, September 1

Good morning from trackside. I'm leaning on the outside rail of the Oklahoma training track, taking in the sounds of Saratoga in the morning. I stand stationary for a change and take in the motion around me at the busiest spot on the backstretch. At the gap of the track as the turf opens in the infield and the morning is in high gear.

This is what I hear . . .

"Cup of tea."

"Be better in a minute."

"Egg and cheese."

"Come on, horse."

"I got half a mile, I think the kid said."

"Come on if you're coming."

"Been here since '65. Moved out of the city then, I fought that war. Nah ah."

"Rail. Rail. Rail."

"Want to school one?"

"I'm here."

"The sun came up."

"No sense complaining."

"Over to the side with that pony."

"You get a time on Affirmed Lane?"

"1:16."

"1:16."

"Thank you. Thank you."

"Lots of time, nothing coming."

"Party Chatter. Five-eighths. 1:01."

"Thanks."

"What's the big deal, it's not like she went down there in 46?"

"Come on, Skiffington."

"Hurry up, Pat."

Railside on the Oklahoma. *(Harlan Marks)*

"That's not easy with this one."

"Reflect the Music going a half on the grass."

"Oh this is going to be hard. Sorry, coming through."

"We're always having fun."

"Ho-back over there."

"Pattering. P-A-T-T-E-R-I-N-G. That was the one in the back."

"Oh, Jesus. Come on, horse."

"Candle in the Dark. Candle in the Dark."

"Brothers going a half on the grass."

"Lorna has her hands full with that one."

"Well, it can only get better."

"You all jumping the big ones?"

"I might just follow you. That OK?"

"Don't get a big run at it, right from there."

"Whoa, not so fast, son."

"You going again?"

"Yeah, but by myself."

"Good idea."

"She went good."

"I tried to get her to the pole relaxed."

"Feels like a turf horse on the dirt."

"Hey Tommy."

"I almost fell off. He skidded across the road and I almost fell right off."

"Go Onn Guster."

"What are you doing over there?"

"Stakes-placed."

"You want a picture with John Campo Jr.?"

"She came off on the pavement over there."

"Just keep an eye on her."

"Get me going a half?"

"Whoa, Daddy."

"Come on, Jock."

"There are more banks in this town than any town in the world."

"Block for block."

"You know history repeats itself. There is no industry here."

"You going on."

"I'm going off."

"Ssspppphhh. Ssspppphhh. Ssspppphhh."

"You have a call in that race?"

"Another cup of tea."

WELCOME TO AMERICA

Thursday, September 2

The dream continues. Phi Beta Doc and Ramon Dominguez. They won the Saranac Handicap on Wednesday.

Life is about dreams. Horse racing is the sport of dreams. Saratoga, that's life and horse racing at their best. Saratoga—Dreamland.

I caught Ramon Dominguez on his way to the jocks' room after his first Saratoga stakes victory. I love asking a guy like that, a 22-year-old jockey at his finest hour, if I can talk to him for a minute. Here's our conversation.

What's it like?

"It's exciting to win a stake anywhere but even more here because you're competing with the best of the best."

It looked like your horse lugged in last time (he finished second in the National Museum of Racing Stakes on August 9 at Saratoga).

"I was going to win the race last time if my horse ran straight. This one releases a little pressure, because you feel like you should win because you're on the best horse in the race. That's what makes the pressure, you know if things don't work out for the best that you'll be taken off."

That was going through your mind before this race?

"No, it wasn't, because I am very confident and these people have been supporting me real good. You just know that it's there. You know?"

Yeah, I'm a steeplechase jockey.

"I know, I've seen you at Delaware. So you know."

Yeah.

Ramon Dominguez drives Phi Beta Doc home. *(Barbara D. Livingston)*

Where are you from originally?

"Venezuela. Do you mind if I watch the replay?"

So we scooted over to the TV outside the jocks' room and watched Ramon Dominguez's dream come true. This time, there was no lugging, just the perfect trip.

We missed the first half but caught the good half, when Phi Beta Doc turned for home with a trucklike hole to go through.

"I'm passing horses, but I still want to take hold of my horse here. I wait and see what John Velazquez is going to do, he's on my outside, and what Pat Day is going to do. Stay on the inside and there was a shot for me to go in between the horses. It opened up beautifully. You have to know that's going to happen. Sometimes it doesn't but . . ."

He smiled, sweat still streaming from under his helmet, and watched himself win his first Saratoga stakes. Now back to the interview.

How long have you been in the States?

"Three years. I rode one year [in Venezuela] with my bug."

Did you ever hear about Saratoga in Venezuela?

"Not really, didn't hear of any track in this country. But as soon as I got to the United States, I was in Miami, I already knew what Saratoga was. It's very exciting to win here. Like a dream, you know."

What would they be saying in Venezuela right now?

"Oh wow. It's crazy because you cannot break in there. My odds were pretty high there in the beginning. I wasn't supposed to be such a nice rider there. Not too many people had confidence in me or the promotion that I came out of. A lot of other riders were doing a lot better than me. With time I got more experience and getting on better horses, things are working out for me. I'm sure they would be surprised and happy for me."

Do you have family down there?

"Yeah, all my family is there."

When will you call them?

"Tonight." With the greatest smile you could ever see. Nothing like making family proud.

What are you going to tell them?

"Oh, they'll know. They have a computer, with the Internet."

Hi, Dominguez family, your boy just made a dream come true. You should be so proud.

BAILEY SPEAKS
Friday, September 3

Who told me I was lucky? Who didn't? That's the one thing I hear: "You are so lucky, doing what you love."

Can't argue there. I was sitting on a curb eating pizza at one in the morning, riding Repeat Peteski at seven, writing about the Breeders' Cup by nine. This is a great life. I'm a little late today. I've been writing an article about riding the Breeders' Cup for *The Florida Horse* magazine. I talked to Jerry Bailey, Pat Day and Mike Smith about riding for $13 million. Another part of my luck, sitting under the trees outside the Saratoga jocks' room talking to legends. Pat Day told me about Wild Again winning the first Breeders' Cup Classic and about his life with and without the Lord.

Bailey talked about the Breeders' Cup and about this meet.

Mike Smith laughed and gave advice on how to ride the Breeders' Cup—stay out of his way and let him through. We talked about having a flat jockeys vs. jump jockeys race series. Wouldn't that be cool? Make the weights 145, three races, one six furlongs on the dirt, one two miles on the turf and one in between. I know the flat riders won't jump the fences but we'd be willing to break out of the gate. Make the races for charity. What do you think? Call the NTRA to get this thing rolling.

Everywhere I go, I am bombarded with more suggestions—no complaints, only suggestions. Talk to Edgar Prado. Stop by and see Kelly Kip. Spend a morning at Bill Mott's barn. That's just the writing suggestions. Come gallop a horse. School this horse for me. Groom that horse better. Find a new grill. Water the plants. Feed the fish. Send me photographs. Talk to me about the publishing schedule. Pick up tack. Come back. Stay there. Do something.

Jerry Bailey.
(Barbara D. Livingston)

I need to get over for the races, too. See Surfside, the undefeated daughter of Seattle Slew and Flanders, run in the Spinaway.

And don't look now but my friend Wass is coming to town for the weekend.

So I give you Saratoga's leading jockey, Jerry Bailey.

"It's been a spectacular meet. The first four weeks were unbelievable. The next eight or nine days I only won three races so it slowed down. I figured to have that happen sometime during the meet. I think I've ridden better at other meets—the year I won 47, I think I rode better, a lot of sitting and getting through on the fence, I won six or seven races that I shouldn't have that year.

"This year I think I've won because the horses were good enough. In the '80s Cordero was the man. I was always the one maybe that was supposed to beat him, because of the outfits I rode for, Rokeby, Greentree, but I never could really seriously threaten him. I think I got within a couple one year. Then Mike [Smith] had his run and I had a good run for four years. I think it's harder—and that's why I tip my hat to Angel—it's harder to win a few in a row because the expectations are so high on you. I could feel the expectations last year and Johnny Velazquez won it and really Mike should have, and I think this year they were on Johnny more than me."

Did you come into the meet with a different attitude?

"In all honesty, I did. Last year I just started playing golf and morning work, as you know, is very important. Last year if there wasn't anything going on at 7:30, quarter to eight, instead of going and looking for something I would go to the golf course and practice. This year I came in more focused; golf was going to take a backseat and I worked a lot harder in the morning. It kept me more focused on what I was doing.

"I don't get on many horses, but just the fact of being out helps. Watching what's going on with the track and people seeing your face—you're around what's going on and other people see you and might put you on a horse that they wouldn't normally put you on."

Any regrets?

"No. I don't think I've made any bad rides. Usually I'll pick out a ride or two that I made a mistake in, when I really thought I could win a race. Maybe riding Yes It's True and not Forestry."

Yes It's True finished last in the King's Bishop. Forestry won with Chris Antley aboard.

That was just part of my brief conversation with Bailey; we talked mostly about the Breeders' Cup. I asked him to name his best Breeders' Cup ride.

"Probably Arcangues [1993 Classic winner]. He came from last and only went around one horse. Concern was good, but Arcangues was the best."

When Bailey says "around," he means outside. He went inside every horse but one. What a vision. What a conversation. Yup, I am lucky.

SIGHTSEEING

Saturday, September 4

I just passed a man running down Fifth Avenue with the newspaper tucked under his arm. He was decked out in his running gear,

Shug's beautiful horses. *(Deirdre Davie)*

looked like he was on the last half, and ready to get home and read the paper. That's what I love about this town, those little scenes inside the big scene.

It might be Rooster smoking a cigarette and reading the program under the trees.

The couple sitting on their Phila Street porch, bottle of wine and a candle, past midnight.

The boy riding his bike through Congress Park with his girlfriend on the handlebars.

The dart boards and dart throwers at the Parting Glass.

Scotty Schulhofer standing on the turn of the main track every morning.

The horses galloping under the trees on Clare Court.

The wait at Sperry's.

The racing show.

The man walking down Nelson reading the *Racing Form.*

Allen Jerkens ambling past on his pony.

Shug's string of beautiful bay horses standing in the courtyard ready to train.

All the Behrens hats under James Bond's shedrow.

The man collecting money at the exit for the Salvation Army.

Moe's coffee truck.

Morning trips to Dunkin' Donuts.

The plaques inside the Hall of Fame.

The statue of Seabiscuit outside it.

The fire station.

The *Saratogian* building on the corner.

Caffe Lena's wooden door.

The ride, downhill, to town.

The ride, uphill, to home.

Grateful Dead sounds bellowing out of Aiko's.

The paper lady singing, "PAAAPERS."

Homemade lemonade stands.

The Reading Room and its stickers.

The American flag in the infield.

Jockeys walking through the crowds.

Photos on the wall of the Wishing Well.

The sign outside the door of the Mexican Connection.

The Five Points Laundromat.

The pure elegance of the Adelphi on Broadway.

The Pink Sheet.

Trying to hit the triple in the last.

The crowds lined up to look at the horses in the paddock.

The gentle rhythm of the lead ponies.

The Spanglish of the backside.

The straw pillows in the front of the stalls.

Crossing Union Avenue first thing in the morning.

Memories of Rokeby Stable.

The temptation of the canoe.

The man playing the banjo on Broadway.

Lawn seats at SPAC.

The faces you see in the crowd.

Even the zings.

"Hey Jerry Bailey, smile, it's not that bad," from trainer Gary Sciacca at the Carving Board counter.

"You're not hungry. I am," from Bailey on his way to ride the last.

Just a quick list of the notes that make the ballad.

The end of Saratoga 1999 is only days away. I'll miss writing these letters every day. Doesn't seem possible that it will all be over and I'll go back to longhand in my journal. When do I stop? I guess I'll wrap it up on Tuesday. The steeplechase crowd heads to Belmont for a race on Friday and then it's back to Unionville, Pa., for the fall, unless something else comes up. In Unionville, you ride horses and read, that's about the extent of activity there.

I can't deny my sadness about it all ending. It's like this every year for me, but I feel much better about it this season. I guess I don't have any regrets this year, at least, professionally. Picture me last year, after not being able to sell my journal idea, all this stuff happened and I couldn't share it; that's the special part of this year, the idea worked. We shared the Saratoga season. That can never be taken away.

FADING

Sunday, September 5

Two days, two nights and a lifetime.

Saratoga is over on Tuesday morning, the end of the racing season. And the end of this chapter in life. Maybe I will be back next year, but I won't be the same. You never leave Saratoga the same person you came. It's just that way for Saratoga people.

We came, we saw, we survived. Some struggled and some flourished. There was no conquering; we never beat Saratoga, and we wouldn't want to anyway.

Love is not jealous, love doesn't keep score, love doesn't play games. Saratoga, too. The town, the racetrack, the people—Saratoga exists in a physical state. But it's Saratoga in all the mystique and majesty that shapes lives. It's Saratoga, the state of mind, the way of life, that makes the difference.

See, the place invokes expectations on everyone. This is where people want to be their best. You can always go home—no challenges, no fears, no surprises. Home is life's crutch, pillow, support system. And Saratoga is the expectation capital of the world.

The fading light. *(Deirdre Davie)*

When I come to Saratoga, I want to be that person who exists only in my head, the one I strive to be. The one being who possesses the confidence, the pride, the peace, the strength to be content. I never find this heroic being, at Saratoga or anywhere else. Maybe Saratoga helped me come close, maybe I drifted further. But I never found the highest rung, and that's the part that makes Saratoga so unsettling.

I still have a mental checklist of things I was going to do. I never made it to the Yaddo Gardens. I never took my beautiful date to Chez Sophie. I never swiped the canoe. I never made it to Cooperstown. I never cashed that big ticket. I never met that one person who was going to change my life. I never sang at open mike. I never reached it.

I'm not alone.

Leaving Saratoga forces you to check. To look around and see where you are. And, of course, where you are going.

When you say goodbye, you look back at the last six weeks and take note of your progress. In turn, you look ahead at the next 10½ months and wonder. Now is the time you face the Saratoga experience. You put clothes you never wore (still in the cleaners bag from home) back in the car. That new suit, that short dress, that spectacle hat—all put away until next year.

That bottle of champagne, that box of cereal, that unopened book—all placed back in the cardboard box in which they came.

That grill, that porch, that dining room table—all barely used over the last six weeks.

The trio of dead plants, the crate of recyclables, the coffee cup full of change—remnants of the binge.

The credit card bills, the mobile phone debt, the pile of old mutuel tickets . . .

Saratoga has come and gone. Two more days to clean up the mess and find a way back to I-87. I'll be on the road by Wednesday, packed up, trying to keep the dry-cleaned wrinkle-free and the rest of my belongings from sliding over my head.

The horse vans will be lined up from Union to Broadway. I'll drive by our host on Union Avenue, she'll look older now, lonely. The red and white awnings won't look so crisp. The paint will look drab-dull brown. I'll notice all the dead grass and the cracks in the concrete. The doors will be locked. All the wooden crates will be packed away. Traffic cops will be a distant memory. The pigeons and the squirrels will get their private home back. *The Pink Sheet* won't be found. Sea Hero will be a solitary object in a yard of matted grass.

Saratoga is on holiday—hibernation.

SINCERELY

Monday, September 6

And on the last day . . . we looked around in all directions, stopped and stared at all the motion, wondered where we should be going and if we'll ever get there.

Good-bye, Saratoga. It seems like I'm the only one still looking at what's here and not what's coming next. Vans clang around the stable area, rooms are being abandoned, dust whirls from all the commotion, horses have a look in their eyes like they might be left

The iron jockeys will stand guard another year.
(Harlan Marks)

behind. Cats scurry, trash cans overflow, old straw piles up in the shedrow. Looks like people can't get out of here fast enough. It never ceases to amaze me how they arrive and how they leave. Back on July 28, it looked like the first day of summer vacation. The place brimmed with high hopes and shades of freedom. Now it's like a tidal wave is on the way, as people disperse with reckless abandonment.

Today is the last day of racing. Shipping Day is tomorrow. I'll be here until Wednesday and then go my way.

The first race of the last day goes off in about 20 minutes. And the last horse of 1999 will cross under the wire in about five and a half hours. That will be it until next July.

The last day will decide the trainer's race. D. Wayne Lukas, Bill Mott, Todd Pletcher and Stanley Hough all have a shot at the title. The jockeys' race has long been over, with Jerry Bailey cruising to his fifth championship. Edgar Prado could catch Jorge Chavez for second. That's your news for today.

We met some fun people and horses, that has been the highlight. I hope you felt like you walked up the stretch with Silverbulletday, cheered on Behrens and Victory Gallop, felt every ache and pain with Succeed. That was the idea.

I know I enjoyed all the good moments more because of relaying them to you. The bad moments, too. When they scanned Succeed's leg, I stood there thinking to myself, "Why did I write all about this horse? Why did I let them in on how I felt about this horse? Now I have to tell them it's over, that it wasn't meant to be, that we failed." But in the long run, I think writing about Succeed was the best part. After a while, I realized maybe that's why he was here and that this was his epitaph. I'm not sure I'm using the word right, the definition says a brief statement commemorating or epitomizing a deceased person or something past. He didn't die, but his career is something past. So maybe me writing my first journal at Saratoga and having Succeed here to play a part in it was what was supposed to happen. That was why I met him. I'll never forget my first Saratoga journal and I'll never forget Succeed.

Every day as I work through my morning, I'm confronted with

this plaguelike dread that I can't write today, like I used all my good words yesterday. It's like this every day, and that's another good part of this journal; I never ran out of words. Maybe I ran out of new or good words at one time or another, but for the most part I kept telling tales.

So off I go for the last day of racing, I'll try not to cry, kick and scream, or picket for a 37th day. Time to move on.

Before I came to Saratoga this year, I dug up my old journals (don't call them diaries) and threw them in my bag of tricks. As the last day comes, I looked back at my final Saratoga entry from two years ago, before Hokan, Succeed, and *Saratoga Days*. Things are definitely looking up.

THE OLD DAYS
September 1, 1997

It's over. And it almost had the perfect ending. Cadence Count defied all laws of form and rallied to finish second to Green Highlander. I rode a good race although I might have moved too soon. I rated him last all the way around, moved through traffic on the turn and then punched at the head of the stretch to come up empty when I landed at the last. Fun ride that fell short, like all my Saratoga '97 rides. I rode some fantastic horses (in heart, not ability) and rode well all meet. Just couldn't win one, and that was my one goal six weeks ago. Two seconds, three thirds, two fourths and two pull-ups. It's all over now. The million-dollar question is, will I be back next year? Part of me (the part who still finds it special to walk out to the paddock after losing four pounds in the sauna) says without a doubt, don't give up on something so special, so rare, so extraordinary. The part who loves being different, doing something that so few can do. The other part (the one who's sick of riding second-string horses, losing four pounds in the sauna, the part that grumbles when Kiser, Kingsley and Miller, C. and B. [Blythe, Chip's sister], win all the races) bows farewell and says I'll never miss you, I'm sorry I stayed so long. Which one will stamp the final decision? I really don't know. I'll miss Mig, Mario and Mike Smith. I love that part, I really do. I just wish I'd win every once in a while. That's the part I can't stand, not being successful. The frustration of being beaten every week by those I know I can ride with, that's the part I'm tired of. Sounds lame, selfish, yes. But it's been a long time. I have no business whatsoever. If I could see a light, that would help the decision process. But at the moment, who's to say it will get better? Hello, tell me it's going to get better. Not that Chip BS of doing the right thing and being tested by some outward, upward being/force who is making me stronger by this struggle that he puts me through. I believed that once back in the early '90s of horses like Flaming Hoop and Rev Three. But now? I think I've wised up to all that fog. I need facts or something tangible. My popularity in the sport has waned to near zero. And it's going down faster and faster. I love the four minutes in the race. I love the unconventional lifestyle. I love the traveling. I love the winning when it happens. But the down side comes with the people, the social life, the frustration . . . and all that. Give me some feedback. Come on pipe up, say something. Anything. I'm waiting. Yeah, yeah, I laugh now. I laugh.

Yikes. I think I had a midlife crisis at 27. The good thing about keeping journals is that you can look back and realize you are a whole lot better now than you were then. Riding races is a great thing, but you don't want to make it everything. It is what it is, the more pressure you put on yourself the harder it is to succeed. Back in 1997, I obviously didn't have much to do. I remember that year. I was depressed that I gave Rowdy Irishman a bad ride in the Turf Writers—man, I lost myself. My family was sorry they came to Saratoga, that's how bad I acted. My girlfriend Annie came to Saratoga to have fun with me. She left thinking I was the biggest fool in the world. And you know, she had a point. She didn't come this year, and that's a shame—I think she would have liked what she found this time.

That might be the tragic part of life, when you finally figure it out, those who suffered through the time you spent figuring are no longer around. You would do anything to show them that it's all different but that moment is gone.

What I now know about me is that if I had fallen off Pinkie Swear at the fifth fence, it would have been a bummer. I would have wished you could have been along for a winning ride. But that's all it would have been. I have come a long way, replacing the significance of winning a race with the significance of being someone. Not a famous someone but a someone inside.

Not sure that's it exactly, but I know that I've come a long way from the time I wrote that dour account of life at Saratoga back in 1997. Things have improved; riding races is exactly that now, riding races. For that, I'm grateful.

I hope in the last six weeks, I gave you an enjoyable trip. That's really all I was trying to do. I guess in what I write, I try to learn about myself and about life at the same time. I'm not sure that works, but that's the theme to all these words. I'm not a genius or a philosopher. I am just me. And this was just me at Saratoga.

I promised you a six-week ride. I hope I delivered.

FAREWELL

Tuesday, September 7

Hold back the tears, this is the last one. The final edition. Good-bye, my friends.

I was told I wrote too much about leaving Saratoga. That's because after the Travers, that's all there is to do. Now I'm writing my last column and spending my last night in town.

Of course, it rained yesterday, thus turning the last day into this surreal final climax. Seems like it's this way every year. The races were off the turf and there was a strange twist in the air.

Crafty Friend and Affirmed Success put on one last horse-racing-is-king spectacle with a seven-furlong battle in the Forego Handicap. They went at it every step in wild fractions with Crafty Friend eventually prevailing by a neck. Just one more show to file away in the Saratoga vault.

I watched the race with Richard Migliore, who would have been riding Crafty Friend. As the horses were loading into the gate, Migliore told me he talked to his replacement Gary Stevens about the horse and that he should suit him well. I asked Mig what he had told him.

"Don't hit him. You can wave it but don't hit him."

So there we were watching the last stakes of the meet in the standing crowd, Mig cradling a broken arm and Gary Stevens hand-riding Crafty Friend to victory. Another bittersweet moment for Richard Migliore in Saratoga Days 1999.

Bill Mott took the trainer title, Jerry Bailey the jockey. Edgar Prado won two more races yesterday to catch Jorge Chavez for second in the jockeys' race.

So it's all over now. We go our separate ways. Thanks for reading.

Gary Stevens waves his whip at Crafty Friend. *(Barbara D. Livingston)*

This day's column is a little like the Succeed story, too grand to be able to write a proper account of it. Saratoga ends every year and it always feels like this. So we let it go, give it time to rest and we'll be back another day.

Saratoga has been good to some and bad to others. I happened to come across a man sleeping in his car this morning. Hatchback wide open with his legs hanging in the wind. Times are tough even at the Spa.

Good-bye, Saratoga, thanks for the memories.

Now I'm going to get some sleep.

Sunset on Saratoga Lake. *(Harlan Marks)*

One More

As I finished this journal through Saratoga, I wanted one more character to sum it all up. I found the perfect person. Richard Migliore.

In the beginning, I mentioned how Saratoga 1999 had taken a hit when Amarettitorun was claimed from Leo O'Brien. Barely a graze, compared to the loss of Migliore to the Saratoga jockey colony. The Mig broke his arm a week before the meet when he took a brutal fall at Belmont Park, another step backward for the 35-year-old jockey who has suffered enough blows in his career to make a punch-drunk boxer feel untouched.

Crash test dummies have had it easier than Migliore, who has risen (the hard way) from teenage backstretch exercise rider to one of the country's finest jockeys. In between, he battled weight (my bouts with the sauna are vacations compared to the Mig's life), injury (he broke his neck in a 1988 fall) and a constant working-man's career as a jockey.

For close to 20 years Migliore has been up and down the ladder but finally in 1999, Migliore's stock—the horses he rides for a living—had reached another level. He spent the winter in sunny Florida instead of in the snow at Aqueduct, riding Saratoga-type horses year-round. Migliore was ready for his breakout season at Saratoga when J. Carson broke his left front cannon bone at Belmont Park a week before the meet. The fall sent Migliore to the ground, the ambulance, the hospital and eventually the bench to contemplate the racing gods.

You can feel sorry for Migliore if you want, but in all the struggles he has achieved something far greater.

I watched him throughout the summer of 1999. As the meet opened he talked about trying to help trainer John Kimmel in the mornings—from the ground rather than the saddle. Later in the season, he showed me the X-ray of his right forearm: two bones, two plates, 16 screws and all. By the end, he rode past me on the back of Kimmel's pony, left hand grasping the reins, right hand useless.

I found Migliore six months later at the Laurel Park jocks' room in the midst of his comeback. I asked him about his life before, during and after Saratoga 1999.

Instantly Migliore reassured me that I needed his story in my book. His story is a long one. I attempted to edit it and eventually decided it's too good to cut. As if we were connected, he opened the conversation with:

> Saratoga is so special. I guess I am somewhat of a romantic anyway, but I remember being a kid up there, 15 years old, living on the backstretch and riding my bike through the neighborhoods. I had read Walter Farley's fictional biography of Man o' War and I'd see people that I knew were owners. I'd go past these grand homes and think about Man o' War's groom walking through the town and think about their conversations talking about horses and racing. I just remember getting so caught up in that spirit. Anytime I go to Saratoga I can walk right back into that feeling. You know, you get older and you get a little more cynical, beaten up, jaded, whatever it is. Go to Saratoga and you can be that kid again with that whole fantasy world going on and yet you get a chance to live it. Saratoga is unique that way, it can always transport you back into that place that makes racing special. That's what it's all about.

Our conversation, which happened on February 20, took us both back to August. Actually it wasn't really a conversation, I just let him talk:

Richard Migliore rides alone on the meet's final day. *(Barbara D. Livingston)*

To ride at Saratoga is a dream. The atmosphere, the excitement in the air, everybody is so into it. Into the horses. The whole event of it all. It's not like a normal day of work, getting up and going to Aqueduct. When you walk out the door in the morning at Saratoga, the sky's the limit. The possibilities, the things that can happen to you are endless. You can turn the corner at Saratoga and walk into the next Seattle Slew.

To me, even as a kid, turning up Union Avenue in a

horse van and poking my head out, that almost carnival-like country atmosphere—but yet it's big money, high society. It's where all cultures meet, everybody's excited about it. The grooms, the hotwalkers, the exercise boys and then you have every big owner and every big trainer there. Everybody wants to win at Saratoga. There is nothing that compares to winning at Saratoga.

It dawned on me about six days after the fall when I got checked out of the hospital that I wasn't going to compete in Saratoga [1999] at all.

Missing the meet hurt. I had never been working as many good 2-year-olds leading into Saratoga, so I was really excited about the meet. It was really discouraging. But the funny thing was I knew I was going there. I knew without a shadow of doubt I wasn't going to stay home on Long Island when all my friends and all the horses that I work with went to Saratoga. I needed to be there in that atmosphere.

But it was tough. It was probably the most frustrating period of my career. When I broke my neck and missed Saratoga years ago, it wasn't as tough on me for a number of reasons. I was so hurt, physically, I was so debilitated, that riding was so far off and missing Saratoga didn't even hurt that much. It was like I just had to get my body back.

This time, yeah I was hurt but it wasn't such an uncertain injury, I knew I was coming back, it was just—damn, I'm going to miss Saratoga. Also I didn't have that many good horses to lose then. I was holding my own, maybe I would have won eight, ten races at Saratoga, but this time I had thoughts of being leading rider.

No one will ever know, but maybe Migliore could have claimed the 1999 Saratoga riding championship—Jerry Bailey's award. Migliore's horses and Migliore's trainers won races throughout the meet. The success didn't escape him.

To see all those loaded guns go off without you. The fact of the matter is at that level any number of guys would get the job done with the horses. There's not a lot separating 20, 30 guys. When you put that gun in anybody's hand, they're going to pull the trigger and get the job done.

I was riding a lot of good horses. That hurts. You sit there and think about all the work you put in. I didn't get to finish the job, but I have the roadmap now. I know how to get there now, I just have to work on it again. Hopefully this year I will be just as strong going into Saratoga.

In 1998 I got beat two winners for the whole thing—and then last year I was loaded. I was working Dat You Miz Blue, I was riding Bevo, I was working Chief Seattle, I was working Regally Appealing, and Dream Supreme for Linda Rice. And then the first day of the meet, four horses that I had the call on won. It was heartbreaking. I tried to keep a good handle on it and appreciate that as bad as I got hurt, it could have been a lot worse.

But the week Regally Appealing won the stake on Monday and Bevo won the stake on Wednesday, I was at my house and I was so frustrated. Something happened and I pulled the closet door completely off the hinges. I still had this arm in the cast. The baby says, "Ohh my daddy's mad." Then you kinda come back to earth when you see what kind of example you're setting.

So I went up and got lost in the Adirondacks for a couple days. It was tough, but you know what? You get through it and you get other chances. Thank God, and hopefully, I'll be back at Saratoga working on it and hopefully be as loaded as I was last year. It's hard though; at this stage of the game you wonder how much work you have to put in to get back to that point again. You don't want to get caught up in the frustration of things, but you hope that it comes back quickly and easily. Although nothing worthwhile is easy, right?

I had mixed emotions when all the horses were winning. You got to feel like, "I wish it was me." But I was helping the people who had helped me before I got hurt, so it was that team mentality, too. Gary Stevens [who rode Crafty Friend] is a good guy—why would you begrudge him or the team? Definitely mixed emotions. You're happy for the players that were involved, but there is still that little bit of feeling sorry for yourself.

Migliore was seriously injured in the Belmont fall. He couldn't ride races for six months. His career could have ended but—and every jockey rides with this—if luck had bounced him in another direction he might not be talking about getting back to Saratoga.

You see a guy like Rudy Baez who has ridden his heart and soul up in New England and never gotten to the level or the opportunity that I've gotten. The guy's a great rider, he's done it through the worst conditions and sometimes on the worst of horses. He's always given 120 percent and you see him take a fall like that and get paralyzed [in an August 4 fall at Rockingham Park] and he's not going to have another chance. That kinda sobers you up from that "why me, poor me" attitude.

It could always be worse; you almost feel a little bit ashamed for feeling sorry for yourself. You know what? This will pass and I'll get over it. You look at his situation and how well he's dealing with it, the pride and courage that he's showing, if people like that can't be an inspiration to you . . .

I think it's just trying to find that balance. You go back and forth but in the long run if you stay even and you try to keep your eye on what's important—it works out. Right now there is such a pure feeling to what I'm doing.

I feel like that kid again that is just so happy to do it, not so caught up in who you didn't get to ride. You're more just happy for what you've got. Human nature. I'm sure there'll come times that I'll say, "Why didn't I get to ride that horse?" I hope not, and right now I don't feel that way. Whatever you have is good and work to make it better. Do the best you can and go forward. If I can do that for the rest of my career, however long it will be, I can walk away and be happy with what I've accomplished, what I've done.

Basically, if I look at it realistically, I had no right to get as far as I did. I came from a home with no horse background, lived until I was 11 or 12 in Brooklyn, New York—not exactly horse country—moved to Long Island where there were some horses that caught my eye, got in with a couple of guys who liked it, too, and the way it just kinda blossomed and I was lucky enough to meet people that were able to help me, and to be in the right place at the right time and to continue to grow and grow.

You think about fate, I think I was blessed with so much God-given ability but the luck of the draw, fate . . . I think in a lot of ways I'm very dedicated but I'm very lucky and very fortunate.

As a whole, I've done a lot more than probably I ever had a right to do. If someone would have said when I first started that I'd wind up being one of the leading riders in New York and that I'd win 3,000 races, I would have signed it right then and there. And I'm not done in a longshot. Hopefully things will just continue to get better.

Other than the real big horse, the Breeders' Cup, the Triple Crown–type races, my career as a whole doesn't lack anything. I've been real lucky to have ridden quality horses for good horsemen and learned a lot. Sometimes I think of some horse that I've ridden that makes me feel good inside. Steamers.

When I am asked how I became a steeplechase jockey, I joke that I had no choice—I was born into it. With my background—(farms, ponies, riding lessons, foxhunting, a trainer for a father)—I couldn't not be involved with horses. Racing found me. Migliore found racing.

I knew I was going to be a jockey when Honest Pleasure got caught by Forego right on the line in the 1976 Marlboro Cup. We had a pony business. We'd go buy ponies cheap from a guy in Riverhead. When I say cheap—$25, $30. They were unbroke, half-broke. We'd take them to my friend's dad's place and break them. The ones that we got bombproof we'd sell to people for their kids for $250, $300, make a pretty good profit. The ones that were bombproof but ugly or no one wanted we'd advertise in the *Penny Saver* for pony rides at parties.

But then we'd always have a couple that were about half-broke or a little wild, so we'd train those for the pony races. We had them trained, they always started the races at the soccer goals. So we'd go out there and school them, practice. Ride short stirrups. When they turned the right way—get out of the way, they were gone. For an eighth of a mile, they could fly. We would pack them full of feed for three days, give them vitamins, not let them out their stalls for a couple of days before the race so they would cut for an eighth of a mile. Kids would show up in western saddles—not us, we had snaffles, short stirrups. I'd put on this black and white sweater that looked like silks.

We had won a race [on Marlboro Cup Day]—it was a big pot, $100 to the winner. So we went back to the barn, it was raining, big heavy turf and the filly had bowed, we broke her down. We got her back to the barn and did her up the best we could—we were just kids. So we put the race on in the tackroom and here comes Forego and Honest Pleasure. And it looked just like the pony race:

she had stumbled at the break, that's where it probably happened, and got up—200 yards and you're four or five lengths out of it, and she got up in the last jump. So we watch Forego with Shoemaker catch Honest Pleasure with Perret right on the money. That day I said, "I'm going to be a jockey. That's what I'm going to do." I had always thought about it, but that day I decided.

We would have three or four ponies in each race and we'd come home and write up charts of the races, "Broke alertly . . ." This was out in Deer Park, Long Island. My friend's dad had a barn and a couple of acres. The Deer Park Pony Association put on these pony races, three or four races, $10 entry fee, winner take all. To this day, I swear, I know it's not possible because she was just a little pony. But she was as fast as anything I've ever sat on for 100 yards. Obviously I've been on a lot faster but when I think of fast horses I think back to her, she could fly.

I think the only race we ever lost was when I was three in front on a pony called Wild Fire and he put his head down and started bucking, sent me flying, so lost rider. Half the time I'd have to run 'em up this hill to stop. We had a blast, then we all left home to go to the farm. David Figuroa, who was Mike Hushion's assistant, and his cousin Carlos, who's training at Aqueduct now. Carlos was going to be the trainer, David and I were going to be the jockeys. We left home and that's what we were going to do. We were 13 years old when we went to Lake View Farm and then Hemp Hill Farm. When I was 14 years old, I hit Belmont Park.

I didn't finish high school then. I wound up going back a few years ago. My oldest was about three or four and I thought, "Man I don't want to lie to the kid when he gets older." I finished. Now I say I went to Belmont Park University.

The university has never had a better student. Saratoga has never had a bigger fan. Like anyone, he remembers his early trips north to the oldest racetrack in North America.

I went to Saratoga in 1980 and thought I was going to get to ride that season but the filly I had been riding in the morning got hurt. The next summer I had been doing great with the bug. I was really loaded with horses at Saratoga. I was going out with [Carmela], who's my wife now; she was Steve DiMauro's assistant trainer and had stayed at Belmont with the second string. We had a big plan: she was going to come up on Monday and we were going to go to an inn in Vermont and celebrate my being leading rider at Saratoga.

I was battling Cordero. I wasn't even driving a car yet, and I was loaded for the last weekend. I won the first race on Sunday and tied it up, 20 wins apiece. I fell in the third race and I was wiped out. Bad concussion, tore my shoulder blade all up. I was in and out of consciousness all day Sunday into Monday, woke up noon on Monday and I started to know what was going on again. I started listening to the races and Cordero hadn't won one all day Sunday so I still had a chance to tie. He wound up winning it with his last ride of the meet, a horse named Great Neck in the Seneca. I remember waking up and Carmela was sitting by the bed; it was a wicked fall, we didn't get to go celebrate anything—that time.

The second time I had a chance was four years later. I was one win behind Cordero and I got days and I deserved them. I always remember what Turcotte said when he took his days and missed Secretariat's last race. "I deserved the days and who am I to undermine the stewards' decision." He was always somebody I tried to emulate for the way he handled himself with so much class, so straightforward. So I took my days, and I definitely deserved them; I was trying a little too hard and I bothered a horse. So the last day I was up there I go out and win four races and go three up. So it was 17 to 14 or something. He ended up beating me a couple of winners. I stuck to my morals, but to what cost?

So twice I had a chance to be leading rider at Saratoga and couldn't do it; but I've had some amazing rides there.

It's really hard to pinpoint any one special Saratoga moment. As an apprentice winning my first $100,000 stake for my contract holder [DiMauro] and breaking Steve Cauthen's money record at Saratoga were two huge events.

Winning the Bernard Baruch on a horse called Win for Sallie Bailey, that was an incredible race. Cozzene, who ended up being turf champion, got a head in front of him coming to the sixteenth pole and he came back and beat him. That to me was one of the bravest performances.

And then the Go For Wand with Hidden Lake, the same kind of scenario. She was in front, a horse collared her and put a head in front of her and she responded and came back and won by a head.

Those kinds of races, at that level, and having the crowd react the way they do. . . . You win one at Saratoga and come back and people are into it. It's not like an anonymous victory—everybody knows about it. Then you walk through town afterward and everybody's patting you on the back. But it's a whole way of life in Saratoga; it's not just go to work and go home.

When you win one in Saratoga you want to savor the moment so much, you just don't want to let it go and just let it pass you by. The moments are too special. Especially when you've got horses that are folk legends, like a Fourstardave or a Thunder Rumble. I've gone a little bit out of the norm and instead of coming back and going right to the winner's circle, I've almost done a little

Richard Migliore and Hidden Lake. *(Barbara D. Livingston)*

victory lap, go up toward the eighth pole, jog along the outside and almost incite the crowd, as much as they're into it already, to get into it more. Drinking in that moment and making it last. You're going to win races other places and be happy about it, but basically you come back and pat the horse, pull the tack off and it's over. Saratoga, it's a moment in the sun, you make it last.

I've already decided, after missing it last year because I was hurt, that I'm going to make them all last. I might be taking a few more victory laps. You realize how precious things are when they're almost taken away from you. To think that, man, maybe I would never ride another winner at Saratoga, and kinda watching from the outside fence—you've got to make every one last without a doubt.

Fourstardave and Richard Migliore, thinking about victory laps. *(Barbara D. Livingston)*

Sounds a little like my conversation with Pat Johnson. Perspective. Maybe it's the injuries, or the constant battle to reach the top, but Mig has more than most jockeys, more than most men.

> The one thing about it is I have a better handle on it than a lot of guys. I understand how precious it is. I see a lot of good riders and very successful people who just don't quite get it. This is an awfully good thing we've got here. It could end at any time. It's all good, that we get to do this.
>
> And it's even better at Saratoga. I've come real close to losing it a couple of times and not getting it back. With this [injury] they told me they might have to go in for the third time and chances are if they do, the chances of me coming back are iffy. When they tell you that, it hits home. You start thinking about if you can't do this any more. What if the last time I rode a horse was July 17 at Belmont Park?

You really struggle with the what-ifs, not wanting to let go of it. Obviously you want to do it and what if you have to stop and what will you do next. If you've never had to struggle with the what-ifs and all the doubts then you don't have a full appreciation of how good things really are. I had to really look at it hard twice. I've taken a lot of spills, but twice the doctors were looking at me and saying "maybe not this time."

I don't want to let go of this; this is great. I get paid a lot of money to ride horses and enjoy myself. I'm into it, I like it. You don't wish ill will on anybody but you would just hope that guys would kinda get it. Guys that are my friends, I love them, but they just don't quite understand how good they've got it. You would hope they would learn through you without having to go through it. Understand it, enjoy this, don't just take it for granted, hop off, pop the girth and walk away. Jog up to the sixteenth pole and feel it.

I thought I was ready to ride in December. I actually was working horses and I went to the doctor on December 29 to just get my OK. He popped it up in there and said, "I don't think you should be getting on horses, let alone riding races, I can't OK you." I still had a 15-percent fracture line and chronic—as long as I still ride races—stress fractures along the screws. "I can't OK you, I think you need another bone graft and I'm not sure you're ever going to get it back."

My next appointment was January 13. I was in such a bad state of mind, I said: I won't get on horses but I'll keep going to the gym, keep my weight, keep doing the therapy. But I had so much anxiety I guess, just worried, over what's my next move if this guy says, "Look this isn't going to work"?

The night before I went to that surgery, January 12, I drove to Belmont Park. It was dark, it was cold. I went to the spot at the quarter pole where I fell, and, I'm not ashamed to say it, I sat there and I prayed. Prayed to God. "Please don't let my career end on this spot. Let me have this back. Thank you for everything, thank you for giving me the 19 years I've had and the life I've had through this and the things I could have never afforded without this but I'm not ready to let go. Please don't make it end on this place right here."

The next day I went to the doctor and he comes in and says, "These are the facts. You have a 15-percent fracture line, it's never going to heal, that's the way it is. With these plates and these screws that's as good as it gets. If you feel strong enough, then I'll OK you, you can do it, that's where I'm at." I said OK, sign it up.

I got on a plane that night and was in Florida getting on horses the next morning and rode six days later. But you just would hope guys appreciate what they have. You want to win, you want to do well, but even when I don't win now, I'm not going home as frustrated or as mad. I was there. Yesterday I rode seven at Gulfstream, I had a couple thirds, it was a tough day but when I pulled up, the outrider says, "Tough day Mig," Not nearly as tough as sitting on the couch watching.

It's all good—I'm competing again. And I'm happy with myself, the job I'm doing, and the way I'm going about things. I don't feel like I'm different. Mentally I'm stronger. Physically I don't think you can stay as good as you are when you're between the ages of 16 and 22, but if you can grow in other areas you can be a better rider or a more complete rider.

I've known you for a long time [Mig was talking to me now], I think we were both kids when we met. Over the last eight years in my life I've probably done the most growing, mentally. Think about the thrills you've derived from riding jumpers, the cool people that you've gotten to meet, and the cool places you've gotten to go. And then the person you've developed into because of the different situations you've had to handle, and handle head on—you can't run away. As a life experience, it's incredible. What a journey. I went from a kid who had never been on a plane in my life to flying all over the place in the first year I was riding. Do you know what it's like to be on the back of a horse and look over at Mt. Fuji and go "How did I get here?" It's because of sitting on this horse. I'm a few years removed from Brooklyn, Sheepshead Bay, and now I'm in Japan because these people want me to ride their horse. This just doesn't happen. This is a fantasy.

If I do win one of those big races, I'll be a blubbering idiot, like Rocky: "Yo Adrian."

If there is a Rocky Balboa in horse racing, here he is, minus the South Philly accent. Mig will be back at Saratoga for the 2000 season, but he never really left. Last year, he watched from the sidelines and still felt like part of the show. The place can do that to you.

Honestly, I can't wait for Saratoga now. It's the one place I can always go and I'm so comfortable there it feels like I'm going home I go by the grandstand and I can really feel the ghosts of racing's past. It just has that unique quality of capturing your imagination. If you ever want to go somewhere and feel the purity of racing, it's all there. The town, the people. Go there in January and you'll find someone who wants to talk about racing. They'll bring up some race or some horse that you rode. I go up there all the time in the off-season. I like to do my Christmas shopping there. I like going up there and feeling a little bit anonymous, but you're never really anonymous.

I remember standing at the three and a half when Affirmed shut off Alydar. I was standing there. Even now I can see the old film and point myself out, standing there watching. Just the fact that you were there. Almost like you're a part of history.

There is nothing like Saratoga—even my kids, Joseph, 9, Philip, 5, Luciano, 2½, get it. They go there and are in awe of it all. They love the place. How did they get it? Just going as little kids and feeling the different atmosphere.

They came to Florida and the baby says, "Dad, this isn't the Saratoga house."

I think what I am showing to my kids is about being a good person, being a strong person. You work hard, you are dedicated, you do face things head on, you are mature, you do handle things correctly and see how far you can go and the person you can be. I think I already see good things in my boys; they are what I take great pride in.

It's almost absurd to think about, but if I could wind up in the Hall of Fame in Saratoga when I finish riding, then my career would be complete. To think that big a few years ago would have been completely absurd, but at this point I think I'm a major-league horse away from having a good shot of that happening. If I could live forever in the most special place of all—in my heart at Saratoga—that would be the ultimate. I think of guys like Jerry Bailey, Pat Day and all the guys inducted there, and for ever and ever, for generations and generations of racing fans, they're going to be there. I can't even imagine—well I can imagine, but I'm sure I can't get the full effect of it. I'd give my eye teeth for it, I know that.

Saratoga 2000. I honestly can't wait to get there and get on horses in the morning. That was tough last year, to be there and not be able to do what I really wanted to do.

There is nothing like getting on horses on a Saratoga morning. The sun just breaking over the top of the trees. The air is so clear. It's just good to be alive.

But I'm going up there on a mission. I know how I am and I know how I'll work through the summer to get to the point that I go to Saratoga as loaded as I was last year.

You want to put on a show up there. You want people to walk around talking about you, telling you that you did a good job. Everybody wants that positive reinforcement, I don't care how old you are, or how long you've done it, it's nice to hear "Good job" and it's even more important to walk away knowing you did a good job. You want to put on your game face and show the world that "This is what I'm about." I'm going to approach it that way. That's how I approached this comeback and that's how I'll approach Saratoga. You know if you're a little run-down, a little beaten up, it seems like Saratoga picks you up. Seems like you work more, you play more and you still have more energy.

A lot of the horses feel that. The odd horse here or there doesn't care for it; maybe the whole thing overwhelms them. Most of them thrive on it. The cool nights, the cool mornings, bright sunshine in the afternoon, the air is so clean.

I think it's a great place for people and horses. If you don't like Saratoga, then you're just pretty down on life. You don't like horses, you don't like racing and you don't like the country.

I do things with my kids up there that at home I just don't have time to do. Everybody's together. You're always rejuvenated at Saratoga.

I remember being a kid living in Brooklyn and getting to go to Lake George for a weekend with my dad in the summer and thinking "Man we're up in the Adirondacks, in the country, in a cabin," and now I get to take my kids up to the Adirondacks for six weeks every summer and I get to go.

I know it will be good to come back and ride next summer because I know how many people will be like, "Man, good to see you, welcome back." People up there are so aware of their racing and what's going on and the fact that I missed last year. I feel like people in Saratoga have always taken me to heart, under their wing a little bit. I've always been embraced by the people of Saratoga.

I went up there in the fall to do a seminar for the Breeders' Cup and the way people talked to me and how good they made me feel: "Can't wait 'til you're back, can't wait to see you next summer." So I know the overwhelming majority will be so pulling for me and happy to see me be back, doing what I do. That feels good, people behind you. That fills the desire to come back and put on a show. You want to leave a legacy. You want to leave there and have people saying, "Did you see Migliore ride Hidden Lake in the Go For Wand?" For years to come that's something that will be talked about.

I remember walking out of the grandstand after that race. He's right. It does leave a legacy. The mystique of Saratoga and its legacy. Mig has ridden thousands of races, but he hopes people remember a handful from Saratoga. He hopes to be remembered for what happened on a few yards of dirt in front of a 150-year-old grandstand.

More than anything else about riding—forget money, forget fame or whatever it is—you leave something behind. You leave people with that thing about you. That you're good at what you do. I guess it's the pride factor. I take a lot of pride in what I do and at Saratoga you know it's appreciated.

It's not like a well-informed but hardcore, cynical Aqueduct crowd. They're great fans and they know what they're looking at, but man they're tough as nails. They don't give you an inch. Saratoga, if you do something good you're the man, and if something happens, beyond your control or not, everybody makes mistakes, don't worry about. They appreciate it. It's just a whole different kind of feeling—again it's the sense of history at Saratoga. It's the fact that I still talk about races up there before I ever rode and "who rode what and what happened." And I know other people are talking about races that I've been in.

Someday I won't be riding races, but I hope that I'm in enough people's minds that they remember me when they think of good riders and people that made contributions to racing in Saratoga. I hope I'm on that list.

I was a kid at Saratoga, 14, living on the backside with a bunch of other guys. We would just make sure we had our loaf of bread and peanut butter for the week in case we tapped out at the races. We'd go up to the clubhouse, see a well-dressed guy and sidle over to him—not that you're doing anything deceptive, but if you've been galloping a horse, or your buddy has, or you know a groom who likes his horse. Give him the inside info so to speak. If the horse wins, you make yourself available and the guy gives you 10 or 20 bucks. So basically you're touting.

We went on doing this and we hooked onto this one guy—we must have given him 10 winners in a row. The guy was great. So one night he says, "I won't be at the races Sunday but meet me for a steak dinner at the Old Fire House. I'll take all you guys for a steak dinner." We're kids, steak dinner, we're living on the backside, this is great. So we show up and we're waiting for him. He comes in and he's got a collar on, he's a priest. We didn't know he was a priest. So now, we're basically all good kids, and we're thinking "what did we say in front of him? Did we talk about girls? Did we curse?" Turns out to be the greatest guy. I'm dear friends with him to this day. Married my wife and me. Christened my three boys. He's like my best friend. This is a relationship that has endured for over 20 years. Father Joe Romano. Father Joe.

In 1985 I proposed to my wife in front of Lyrical Ballad. I had won the stake that afternoon with BC Sal and we were walking toward the restaurant. I had this whole thing planned, totally romantic. I couldn't take it—that ring was burning a hole in my pocket. I just stopped and asked, "Will you marry me?" Now I take my kids to Ben and Jerry's and I look up there and say, "You know I asked your mommy to marry me right there."

Saratoga has a lot of history and has taught me a lot. It's an integral part of life.

Kids go to school in September. We go to Saratoga in July.